MW01165826

MANY CALL ME FATHER, BUT MY KIDS CALL ME DAD

THE LIFE STORY OF A MARRIED CATHOLIC PRIEST

Rev. James E. Lovejoy

Bloomington, IN  Milton Keynes, UK

authorHOUSE®

AuthorHouse™
1663 Liberty Drive, Suite 200
Bloomington, IN 47403
www.authorhouse.com
Phone: 1-800-839-8640

AuthorHouse™ UK Ltd.
500 Avebury Boulevard
Central Milton Keynes, MK9 2BE
www.authorhouse.co.uk
Phone: 08001974150

First published by AuthorHouse 2/13/2007

ISBN: 978-1-4259-8450-2 (sc)
ISBN: 978-1-4259-8449-6 (hc)

Printed in the United States of America
Bloomington, Indiana

This book is printed on acid-free paper.

Song lyrics from "Into Your Hands" copyright Ray Repp.
Quotation from the book "The Prophet" copyright Kahil Gibran.
Song lyrics from "Today" copyright Randy Sparks

I wish to dedicate this story of my life
to those who inspired me to write it...

to my wife, Jackie, my three children, Jennifer, Jon and Jeffrey,

and to CITI Ministries for enabling me to resume ministering to those Catholics and others who, like myself, have been marginalized by the institutional church.

TABLE OF CONTENTS

FOREWORD

My father is the greatest man I know. He's the first man I ever looked up to and the man I've learned the most from. He's taught me more than anyone else and has been there whenever I needed him—and even at times when I didn't think I needed him.

My father is the most caring, honest, nonjudgmental, considerate, generous, and loving man I know. No matter what he's done in the past thirty-four years of my life, he has put his family first. He's also the bravest man I know, and his humility and modesty make him stronger than anyone else. He's made great sacrifices and his life is the one I strive to compare mine to. Someday I hope to find and marry a man who has even half the qualities that my father has.

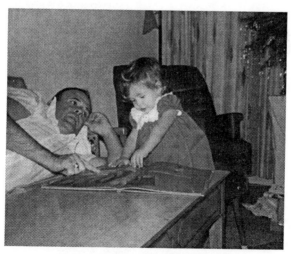

Dad and Me, age 2, 'reading'

All my life, I've known that my father was special. He's made many life choices and has stood by every one of them, dedicating his life to serving God and others. He did an enormous amount of soul searching and praying to choose his career and to fulfill his dreams. His calling allowed him to help countless thousands of people and to make a positive difference in the world. His career may have shifted away from its original design, but in many ways it has come full circle in that a half a century after he started, he's now more qualified, experienced, and educated (both academically and socially) to dedicate many more years to his dream and vocation.

My father is an ordained Roman Catholic priest. He's been married to my mother for thirty-five years and is the father of three grown, successful children. He's also a priest who **has** the joy of four loving grandchildren who would do anything for him. He has the security of knowing that he'll always have the understanding and faith of his family.

This book is the story of my father's life and a testament to the good and positive things one man can accomplish. It's the story of a man who dedicated his life to God and also created a wonderful family that shares his faith and beliefs. He's had many disappointments and turns in the road that he wished could have been different. There are times he felt so low that he questioned his choices, but his faith in God and the love of his family helped him continue to face life's challenges. As I've grown older, I've become even more aware of just how amazing and extraordinary this special man really is.

When my father first wrote a brief autobiography of his life for his children, he was only doing it as a way of sharing what he thought we'd want to know about his life. He didn't plan it to become something anyone else would see, and he laughed the first few times I told him he should write a book.

He kept saying, "Why would anyone want to read about me?"

He didn't think he'd done anything extraordinary, but I've spent years convincing him that his story needed to be told because it would inspire many others to be brave and to do what their hearts tell them to do.

There are people who don't think my father should have left the celibate life as the priest of a Wisconsin university Newman Center to marry and have children. Those same people have families of their own, yet condemn my father for wanting the same thing. He always wanted to help others, to counsel and to minister to them, but he also wanted the love that only a wife and children could bring.

Dad and Jenn at Kineo Mountain, Maine

I'm helping my father write this book to show others that what he did was incredibly *right* and that in a time when many things are going wrong for the Catholic Church, my father is an example of the kind of good the church can do. It's only been in the last few years that people have begun to openly question things the Catholic Church does, and to do so while still saying that they believe in the Catholic religion.

Many people have questioned the Catholic Church for centuries, of course, but when things didn't change, they either left the church or branched out on their own. However, people like my father don't want to leave the church. They want to see the Church change and adapt to it's people's needs.

My father was meant to minister, to guide, and to help other people. When he said goodbye to his congregation at the Newman Center, he told them that he'd spend the rest of his life looking for ways to help change the mentality of the church. He'd try to get the church to understand that people need priests who are one of them, who can understand their troubles, and who can sympathize with their problems. They don't need priests who've had to separate themselves from everyone else and live lives that go against human nature.

There's a growing group of people who are peacefully helping to fight for those changes. It's brave people like my father and my mother who must speak out, tell their stories, and make a difference. It will mean alienating themselves again, but people like my father think it's worth the sacrifice.

As a young child, I thought the fact that my father was a priest and my mother had been a nun was something we weren't supposed to talk about. My parents didn't bring it up when meeting new people and I didn't tell my friends. I thought my parents didn't want to talk about it and didn't want me to talk about it outside of our home.

What I didn't know was that it hurt my parents not to talk about it and not to share their background with everyone they met, but they knew that most people wouldn't understand and that it would be easier for us children in school if it wasn't mentioned. My parents never told us not to talk about it, and I think they would have been upset if they'd known that I was afraid to talk about it. I'd learned not to say anything because of where I grew up, including my community, church, and society in general.

As a child, you don't want to be different—you only want to fit in. My parents' backgrounds were very different from my friends' parents, and I learned it was better not to say anything. However, as an adult, I'm proud of my parents and of their life choices. After all, if they hadn't been so brave, my brothers and I wouldn't exist.

I know that right now is the perfect time for this story to be told, because the Catholic Church desperately needs to be associated with something good. There are many things the church should be ashamed of and needs to apologize for.

Luckily, there are many good priests who are still working to do good things in their communities. Unfortunately, many of them are overwhelmed and underqualified to handle the needs of their congregations because of two factors: they can't relate to the people, and they can't handle the size of their congregations.

They can't relate because they don't know what it's like to be unemployed or to lose their savings through bad investments. They can't relate when parents lose a child because they haven't experienced fatherhood. They can't minister to a couple who wants a divorce because they haven't had to find ways to work through the trials of marriage themselves and don't know how to compromise in a relationship.

There are many priests who are good, kind, honest, and wonderful ministers to their congregations, but they could be even better if they were allowed to experience the joys of having their own families.

There's a huge group in the United States of men (former priests) and women (former nuns) who are missing the joy of serving both God and a congregation. They worship and pray and talk together in small groups all over the country and have only begun to do something to recapture the vocation they miss so much over the past few years. My mother and father are two of those people and have already done some wonderful things with their backgrounds and training.

This book isn't just meant to talk about my father's religious choices. Part of what makes him so extraordinary is that he's made many choices that other people would have been too afraid to make. When something hasn't worked out the way he wanted, or even if it didn't work out at all, he's jumped back in and found something else he could do.

My father's story is meant to illustrate the types of changes that need to take place within the Catholic Church and the people it serves. It's meant to reveal a lifetime of trying to maintain that careful balance between failure and triumph—through the eyes of my father. I hope you'll see how special his story is—and will come away feeling that change is a *good* thing when it happens to and is brought about by good people for the right reasons. It also describes how mistakes can ultimately lead to success and that there's a purpose for everything we do with our lives.

Dad and Me at Moxie Falls, Maine, 2002

My father might not agree about how special his life and contributions have been, but the many lives he's touched are proof that they have been special indeed. When you read his story, there will be times that you'll be able to relate to what he went through, and other times when you'll have no idea what it was like. If nothing else, I hope that Dad's story will help you be more open-minded and understanding of the priesthood and the many pressures it contains—even without the added suffering of having to be celibate for life.

Whether you're Catholic or not, you'll see how important these issues are and the need for change. Allowing Catholic priests to marry would revive the Catholic Church and bring it closer to the religions that have separated away from it over the centuries.

When you need a priest or minister to talk to, it seems only natural that you'd want someone like the man my father is today—not the man he was in his twenties, with little life experience or understanding of life's struggles.

My father's the greatest man I know—the first man I ever looked up to. He's the man I've learned the most from and has taught me more than anyone else. He'd always been there whenever I needed him, and even at times when I didn't think I needed him. He's the most caring, honest, considerate, generous, and loving man I know. He's the bravest man I know and his humility and modesty make him stronger than anyone else. He's made great sacrifices and has lived a life that I'll always strive to compare mine to.

The man I've just described is the type of person who's *meant* to minister to others.

I love you, Dad,

Jennifer

CHAPTER ONE
MY BEGINNINGS

As I begin my story, I'll admit that I have little worldly wealth to leave my family, but I would like to leave them (and others) a legacy of sorts. I have reached the half-century mark of my priesthood and the 35th anniversary of my marriage.

These two vocations are the sum and substance of my life of almost 78 years. I see them as intertwined and supportive of each other. For thirty years after my marriage, my priesthood was more or less inactive, but during the past five years, through association with CITI, a society of married priests, it has come alive again.

My family, especially, my wife and daughter, have strongly encouraged me to write this autobiography. They insist that my story, as well as those of others in similar circumstances, is needed today in order that the church (as the people of God) can better understand the Catholic priesthood through the eyes of those who have been marginalized by an institution that has lost eye contact with those it was ordained to serve.

Someone has wisely said, "It's always best to begin a story at the beginning," so I'll take those sage words to heart and go back to my earliest recollections.

My story begins in 1928, a period almost midway between two World Wars and at the very threshold of a worldwide economic depression. Like the creation of renowned artist Walt Disney's first and most famous animated character, Mickey Mouse, I came into the

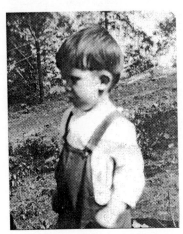

Jim at age 2, 1930

world with little fanfare, the second son of George and Marie Lovejoy in Saugus, Massachusetts.

One of my first and most vivid memories is of an event that occurred when I was barely four years old. My younger brother, Richard (or Dickie, as he was fondly nicknamed) caught a bad cold on a trip the family made to nearby Lynn to purchase Christmas gifts. As the cold worsened and his fever rose, my parents took him to Lynn Hospital for observation. It was there, only a few days later, that Dickie died of a streptococcus germ (a disease that would today be easily cured with an injection of penicillin).

My recollection is that we were all gathered in the dining room of our home when my father received the sad news over the telephone. I was too young to fully comprehend what had happened, or even to be aware that I'd never see Dickie again—at least in this lifetime. He was two years old.

That first sad memory was deeply imbedded, as I learned in years to come, and it had such a profound impact on my father that, according to my mother, he was never the same after

Dickie, George, and Jim circa 1932

Dickie's death. My parents grew apart after that and by the time I was thirteen, they had separated permanently.

My early years, for the most part, were happy ones. I enjoyed the summer trips we took to my uncle's camp at Bear Island on Lake Winnepausaukee, New Hampshire. It was there, I think, that my parents were happiest and spent the most time together. I remember one year, my parents and my older brother, George, and I, stayed at an old hotel in Weirs, New Hampshire (before going over to the island). It was the same hotel my folks had stayed in during their honeymoon some years earlier.

Family Portrait 1931 left to right Jim, George, Mother (Marie), and Dickie

I remember hearing the lonely sound of a train whistle as the Boston and Maine passed almost under our windows during the night. The Moore's Hotel, named after its owner, has long since been replaced by a modern carnival center, but it will always remain in the recesses of my mind.

Another memory of the lake, not quite so nostalgic but vivid nevertheless, is of something that happened during one of our trips from Lovejoy Sands (no relation to our family) in Meredith to Bear Island. In those days, there was very little transportation to the islands on the lake. Even motorboats were scarce, so my father would row the family out to the island, probably two or three miles. That took some muscle, believe me!

About halfway from the dock, we heard a boat whistle and then to our dismay, around the bend of an island appeared the cruise ship, *Mt. Washington* (an old one, side-wheel and all, which later burned in 1939). We were directly in its path. We all started yelling and waving towels and sweaters. Just when we thought we were doomed, the captain caught sight of us and veered out of our way, but the waves from that ship almost capsized our little rowboat. My mother was terrified, since she couldn't swim, and vowed never to get into a boat with my father again.

1939 World's Fair – New York, left to right -friend, May Mcguire, Dad (George), Mom (Marie), George, and Jim

Other memories of my parents and George that have remained in my subconscious over the years include early Sunday morning trips in winter to a nearby hill where my dad would take us skiing (no fancy equipment—just rubber straps over the toes of our shoes as we braved the "cold morning air and the treacherous slopes"). My mother insisted that he have us back in time for Sunday Mass, so our ski outings were never very long.

Then there were the all-day trips with our dad to the rifle range. Dad was a member of the National Guard and his company had monthly tours to a place where they could practice shooting at huge targets that would come up out of the ground as someone would shout, "Mark 1" or "Mark 2." As we grew older, it was a thrill to be able to go down into the pits where the targets were raised. The highlight of those trips was the box lunch we shared with Dad's company members.

George and Jim in the family car, 1932 Pierce Arrow

One of my favorite memories is of a trip we made as a family to western Massachusetts along Rt. 2, which is still called the Mohawk Trail. It was the original path that the Mohawk Indian tribe made famous. In those days, there was very little commercialization and we could imagine Indian braves behind every hill. The highlight of that trip was our overnight lodging at the same farmhouse where my father had worked many years earlier during his youth. Some of the same family members still lived there and remembered him, which made us proud.

All our lives changed dramatically on Sunday, December 7, 1941. Like most people of my generation, I can recall exactly where I was when the terrible news came. My father was in the Carolinas on maneuvers with his division (the old Yankee 26th). In January of that year, amid rumors of war, the National Guard was federalized, making them part of the United States Army. George was sixteen and I was thirteen when the Japanese bombed Pearl Harbor.

George came running into the house to tell us the awful news. My mother and I were stunned, since none of us even knew where Pearl Harbor was. We didn't even think about our father being on maneuvers and what that news would require of him. It wasn't until the next day, when President Roosevelt addressed both houses of Congress and declared war on Japan and Germany, that its full impact hit us. We were at war! Little did we realize then that our dad would be in the South Pacific for the next four years and that we'd see little of him in the interim.

The maneuvers ended abruptly and my father's unit returned to Massachusetts. The last time we saw him for the next few years was late in December at a Howard Johnson's restaurant in Saugus. He came to say goodbye and to introduce us to a friend, Marion Dunham, who would in time become his new wife, even though he could never persuade my mother to grant him a divorce.

Needless to say, all of that had a profound impact on me, although George didn't appear to be that affected. He had his own plans for the future and was already formulating the next steps he'd take. I, on the other hand, knew that I had four years of high school ahead of me and that I'd be needed at home. George finished his junior year of high school and then, in January 1943, he joined the Navy, was granted a war diploma and was soon off to boot camp, never to return to live with us at home again.

My next four years were lonely ones. I had a few close friends, but didn't participate much in school activities. I tried to be of help to my mother, who was heartbroken by my father's desertion. She never got over it and it pained me to see her so unhappy. Secretly, I know that I blamed her for my father's leaving the family. I thought that she was somehow responsible for his leaving. It was a terrible mistake on my part, but at the time I was too confused to think straight and wanted to blame someone—besides him.

While the war was still going on, I thought about quitting school, lying about my age, and entering the service, but the closest I came to doing that was joining the Massachusetts State Guard. At that time, it was made up mostly of men too old for the service and a few kids, like me. I worked after school and during the summers at varied jobs in restaurants and hotels, and even did a stint as a tack welder in one of New England's shipyards.

During World War II, I watched as many of my friends enlisted in the Navy while I was finishing high school. I have many good memories of the years before everyone went their separate ways.

My social life was very limited, especially as it related to girls. I was quite shy and didn't have the courage to ask anyone for a date. I just kept to myself most of the time and, as the school year book described me: "Jim is a very good-looking fellow. We don't hear much from him, but he always seems to keep busy."

I really missed having a dad around and continued to idolize him from a distance. To say the least, my high school years weren't happy ones, and my future was a mystery—even to myself.

Ironically, I finally began to come out of myself in the last few months of my senior year. The war had ended the previous year (August 1945) so it was no longer a major option for me to enter the armed services—although most of my male classmates did. In fact, most of them were in and out of the service before the next war began in Korea in 1950.

I had my first few serious dates in the spring before graduation, including a girl I'd had a crush on since eighth grade. But then everything changed for me—and for my future.

CHAPTER TWO
HOW SHALL I SERVE GOD?

I had been an altar boy during my early years and although I never attended a Catholic parochial school, I was somewhat religious (probably *scrupulous* would be a more accurate description). I felt a need to try to do something that might bring my mother and father together again. With a great deal of trepidation, I decided to talk to my parish priest.

I made an appointment and we had a lengthy discussion about my concerns and my future. He asked if I'd ever considered becoming a priest. I honestly said that I hadn't. He suggested I read a book that he loaned me. It was entitled *When the Sorghum was High*. It didn't sound very exciting, but I said I'd read it and come back in a few weeks and talk to him again.

The book was about a Maryknoll missionary. (Maryknoll is a religious society which trains young men for the priesthood.) As I recall, that priest had been ordained in the early 1920s and was assigned to a mission territory in China. He labored for many years among Chinese peasants, caring for their souls and their bodies. The people loved and respected him very much, but while serving one of the many missions he was responsible for, a group of bandits captured him, tortured him, and tried to make him denounce his Christian faith. He refused, and they put him to death. Maryknoll considers him a martyr to the faith and holds him up as a model for aspiring seminarians.

I was very impressed and during my next visit with my parish priest, I told him so and said that I'd like to join Maryknoll. I felt a calling to the religious life and felt that maybe I could in some way atone for my parents' broken marriage—and perhaps even bring them back together.

I mention that episode because it reveals much about me at that time of my life, when I was searching for meaning and purpose. The parish priest who started me thinking about the priesthood was transferred while I was still in school and another new young curate took his place. He was a friendly, good-natured priest, and helped me make a very difficult decision—to join Maryknoll and to leave soon after graduation for my first year of studies.

My mother was ecstatic. She had no idea I'd ever given the priesthood any thought. My father, who had left the church after becoming a convert prior to his marriage to my mother, was also supportive, even though he had hoped that I might make the army my career. I don't recall how my brother felt, but George wasn't surprised. I think he always felt that I'd do something special with my life.

Emotionally, however, I was still very conflicted. On the one hand, I believed that I had a calling to that life and was prepared to give up any thoughts of love and marriage, but on the other hand, I'd finally found a young woman I deeply cared for and wanted to get to know her better.

We went on what was to be our last date, a movie in the next town, and while walking her home from the bus, I told her of my decision. I know she was hurt and confused since, as a non-Catholic, she couldn't understand how I would willingly make such a strange commitment, yet she told me she understood and admired my decision.

Unfortunately, the priest who was my mentor happened to drive by at that moment. He slowed down and looked at me disapprovingly.

The next morning when I appeared in the sacristy to serve his Mass, his only comment was, "Who was that woman I saw you with last night?"

Then he shook his head in mock disgust. I was dumbfounded and felt terribly guilty, as though I'd committed a great sin. That simple incident stayed with me for years and I believe it colored my relationship toward women for years into my priesthood. He'd missed an opportunity to stop and talk with us and get to know a young woman who meant very much to me. In many ways, his attitude reflected that of the church hierarchy today—very condescending and judgmental!

High School Graduation, June 13, 1946, Saugus High School

I left home during the summer of 1946 after graduating from high school and entered a preparatory program in Brighton, Massachusetts. Actually, I ended up spending the following school year there, since I needed to catch up with other students who had attended Catholic schools. I took classes in Religion, Latin (at that time, the language used by the church), a modern language (French) and whatever other studies would prepare me for first year college in the seminary.

One of the major mistakes I detected while in that *junior seminary* atmosphere was the acceptance of not only high school graduates like me, but also of returning servicemen from World War II. Those men were older and far more experienced in the ways of the world. Many had seen action on the battlefield and had grown up in a hurry. Some were 8–10 years older than the rest of us, yet the faculty treated them the same and expected them to fit in with children like me, barely out of puberty. The fact that so many of those veterans left the seminary during that year was an indication that they felt as if they were being treated like children.

In the fall of 1947, I traveled to Lakewood, New Jersey, where I joined the class of 1951, which had entered its freshman year. I was happy to finally be among people my own age and at last starting my nine-year course to ordination in the Maryknoll Society. We were the first class enrolled in Lakewood, which had formerly been a private college for boys. (The idea of co-ed education was still years away.) Just down the road was an all-girl college. Of course, we were forbidden to go near that school or associate in any way with its students.

That was our first introduction to the celibate life! The girls, on the other hand, were very excited about our presence. They envisioned dances and dates and who knows what else! Their excitement soon turned to disappointment and resentment when they were told that the new school was a Catholic seminary.

I recall that our first year was almost a total disaster. During the first week after our arrival, some of us were assigned to set up the new school and make it ready for studies. I worked on a truck, carting away boxes and debris. We worked until noon the first day and were relieved by another crew in the afternoon. A young man from Queens, New York, who occupied a bunk in the same barracks where I was billeted, took my place on the truck.

Later that afternoon, we learned there'd been a serious accident. The crew had been removing large cardboard mattress covers from the dorms and the young man was trying to hold them down, but a strong wind blew them backward and knocked him off the truck. He struck his head on a rock and died on the way to the hospital.

I remember going through his belongings trying to get them ready for packing. I hardly knew him, but I realized that it could very well have been any one of us. That was one of my closest encounters with death, and it left me pretty shaken up.

Another incident that first year almost closed the school, but somehow we all managed to get through it. We had many boxes and barrels of dry goods that needed to be opened and stored for the feeding of our large class.

One morning during breakfast, a number of seminarians suddenly began choking and a few became quite sick. They were taken to the infirmary and then, when it looked as if they'd contracted food poisoning, they were rushed to the nearby hospital in Lakewood. All of them survived, but they were critically ill for several days.

Somehow, one of the barrels containing sugar had gotten mixed up with one holding lye. Then the sugar bowls on many of the tables accidentally had been filled with lye. Those who had put what they thought was sugar on their cereal were the unlucky ones. Of course, they tasted the lye immediately, but not soon enough to avoid getting some of it into their system.

It could have been a tragedy of giant proportions, but luckily none of those affected had eaten enough to do serious harm to their mouths or stomachs. However, it did cause a few students to have second thoughts about staying at the seminary, and some parents insisted that their sons return home immediately. It took a great deal of persuasion and assurance that nothing like that would ever happen again to eventually bring them back.

Those two incidents taught us a valuable lesson: initiating a new program at a new site can be confusing and downright dangerous. It also made us very much aware of how easily mistakes can be made and how fragile our lives are. Fortunately, nothing like that happened again and we were soon too absorbed with our studies and the seminary routine to think more about it.

We spent three years at Lakewood, leaving only for vacations home at Christmastime and during the summer months. Our first two years were devoted to basic liberal arts college courses. The last two years, we studied philosophy. I remained at Lakewood for my first year of philosophy, but then Maryknoll sent some of the class to Glenn Ellyn, Illinois, for their final year while the rest of us were assigned to the major seminary in Ossining, New York. There we completed our philosophy courses, along with older seminarians who were completing their four years of theology.

The major seminary at Ossining was an imposing structure built mostly of stone and reminded us of the medieval castles in Europe that we'd only read about. It was perched atop a high hill overlooking the mighty Hudson River, just a few miles down river from the U.S. military army officer training school (known to everyone as West Point).

A good relationship had been developed between the academy and Maryknoll over the years. It became a tradition for the Catholic members in each graduating class at West Point to spend a weekend retreat at the seminary during their senior year, and for deacons (students in their last year before ordination) to spend a weekend at West Point. Someone once referred to Maryknoll as the *West Point of the Catholic Church.*

While I was studying at Maryknoll during my second year of philosophy in 1951, we had a special treat one evening. Actually, it wasn't until many years later that I realized what a privilege it was. The Superior General had occasion to meet many famous people in his capacity as head of the Maryknoll Society.

We were told that he had a special treat for us and that both seminarians and faculty were invited to a concert in the dining room. When we arrived for the concert, we were introduced to a lady and her family of ten children, all dressed in Austrian attire. What we heard was the most remarkable evening of beautiful music I've ever experienced. I'm not sure how much we were told about their background, but I soon forgot about it until some fifteen years later, when I attended a new movie release called *The Sound of Music*.

The lady was the Baroness von Trapp, and her delightful family was the Trapp Family Singers, who were portrayed in the 1965 Academy Award-winning movie, which depicted their life and their harrowing escape from Nazi-occupied Austria during the Second World War. The music in that film was the same music we'd been privileged to hear many years earlier. That film was later to become my daughter's favorite—so special to her, in fact, that she named her two Labrador dogs Gretl Edelweis and Leisl, after two of the von Trapp family members.

Another incident at Maryknoll that I recall with some humor was the requirement that we, as seminarians, had to take recreation outside after our evening meal, despite the weather. During the winter months, it could get bitterly cold in Upstate New York. We dressed warmly for our outside recreation, but often found it difficult to keep warm.

Somewhere I'd come into possession of a large Sherlock Holmes-style pipe and although I wasn't a smoker, I'd light it up and suck on it until the bowl almost radiated with heat. Then we'd huddle around that bowl and take turns cupping it with our hands just to feel some momentary warmth. Many years later, when asked by someone filling out forms on our health whether or not I had ever been a smoker, I'd decline to admit my momentary lapses of puffing away on that pipe!

After the completion of philosophy, we received our Bachelor of Arts degrees. Since Maryknoll was still in the process of receiving college accreditation, in those days we received our degrees from New York University. Then, after summer vacation, our whole class traveled to Bedford, Massachusetts, where we were to undergo a year of spiritual development in a very restricted—almost monastic—environment. There would be no visits home during that year and only a limited number of visits from family and friends.

That was called our *novitiate* year, sandwiched between philosophy and theology. The novitiate was actually a kind of vacation from academic studies and allowed us much more time and more opportunities to develop our spiritual lives. It also provided more opportunities to engage in sports, to perform manual labor, and to get to know all our classmates.

My Novitiate year, Bedford, Massachusetts, 1950

There were approximately seventy of us in that class (a huge number in relation to today's small classes). Since Vatican II (1962–65), classes have shrunk, until today only a handful of vocations to the priesthood are ordained—even in the largest American dioceses. Most Catholics today are acutely aware of this phenomenon, but that's a subject I'll reserve until later in my story.

Following our novitiate year, we returned to the major seminary in Ossining, New York, to begin our final four years of seminary training in theology. That would be our immediate preparation for the Catholic priesthood. We had such profound-sounding studies as Dogmatic Theology, Holy Scripture, Moral Theology, Ascetical Theology, Homiletics, and Liturgical Studies. (In retrospect, I believe that it's unfortunate that we didn't have more training in subjects such as Social Justice, Holy Matrimony, Human Suffering, and Courageous Laity.) It was the grasping of those realities around us that should have formed us into caring priests. Perhaps if the church had allowed our preparation to have more of a human face, the moral tragedy concerning pedophilia (and the worse tragedy of covering it up by the hierarchy) would never have taken place.

One of the lasting memories of my first year of theology at the Knoll (as we called the major seminary) wasn't about what took place there, but about an incident that took place a mile or so away, at Ossining's waterfront. Ossining, was (and still is) the location of the infamous New York State Penitentiary. Our sociology class visited Sing Sing, and I was moved by the starkness and foreboding atmosphere of that prison. We knew that only the most hardened criminals were housed there and we knew of the execution chamber (or death house, as it was called), which had been the subject of any number of cops-and-robbers films of the 1930s, 40s, and 50s.

As we walked through the prison and viewed the inmates in their cells and at work, I was struck by the hopelessness on their faces and the anger in their eyes. We were shown the electric chair, where hundreds of death row inmates had met their fate. Some seminarians wanted to sit in the chair (I suppose so they could brag about it to their friends at home), but I had no such desire—only a deep sadness as I considered man's inhumanity to man. The sight of that torture chamber has remained vivid in my memory to this day.

It was during my first year of theology that I learned of two young men on death row who were scheduled to die in the electric chair while we slept in the seminary. The two had been convicted of taking part in the murder of a New York policeman. One of my classmates had gone to school with one of them and prior to the day of execution, he was allowed to visit that young man. He never discussed that meeting, but I knew it had troubled him greatly. On the night of the execution, there were to be four individuals put to death, starting at midnight, one every half hour. None of us could sleep that night. We were awake and conscious of the effect those executions had on our electric power, well over a mile away. Each time the switch was thrown, all the lights in the seminary dimmed, and we knew that someone was dying.

Aside from the two young cop killers, the other death row inmates were much more notorious. They were Martha Beck and Raymond Fernandez, otherwise known as the Lonely Hearts Killers. They'd been responsible for the deaths of many middle-aged women that they'd lured to them by false promises that they'd be meeting eligible men who were looking for marriageable women. Beck and Fernandez then robbed and killed those women. It was one of the most bizarre killing sprees of the day and garnered enormous amounts of publicity.

That episode in our neighborhood had a profound influence on all of our lives. I doubt that many of those young seminarians have ever forgotten that night—even after nearly a half century.

I was never ordained at Maryknoll, nor did I ever go to the missions. At the end of my first year of theology, I was called into the rector's office and told quite bluntly that he'd consulted with others on the faculty, especially my spiritual director, and it was unanimously agreed that I should be dismissed and sent home. They believed that I didn't have the proper disposition to serve on the missions. I was too introspective and lacked the emotional stability to risk sending to faraway lands where I might not have the companionship of my countrymen and would thus have difficulty dealing with other cultures.

Despite my protests, they insisted that it was for my own good—and that the decision was final. So, after seven years of study with Maryknoll, I had been dismissed and was asked to leave the next day. I was heartbroken and my feelings of failure were reinforced. That was the longest trip of my life, but I finally arrived home and tried to explain to my mother what had happened. While she was extremely disappointed and somewhat angry with the seminary officials, she accepted it as God's will and prayed that I'd do the same.

I've had other disappointments, but the dismissal from Maryknoll was one of the worst moments of my life. I couldn't believe that within three years of ordination, my greatest dream had been crushed forever (or so I thought at the time). I had many misgivings and regretted that I'd admitted my concerns and worries to those in authority. If only I could have had one more chance to prove myself. But, unbeknown to me at that moment, God was making a correction in my life, which would include benefits that would only become evident to me many years later.

The following months were difficult. I was twenty-five years old and although the Korean War was over, the draft had continued and I was now subject to being drafted. I tried to pass the exam for OCS (officer training), but my math and science skills were poor, so I reconciled myself to being called up for the army in the fall.

In the meantime, I tried to fit in to the life I'd left after high school. I dated some, but I felt like a fish out of water. I didn't know what to do with my life. My dreams of being a missionary were over, and there didn't seem to be any hope for the future. My feelings of inadequacy were doubled and I fell into a deep depression.

Then, the priest who had guided me during my admission to the seminary after high school came to visit. I don't remember how he found out about my departure. Perhaps my mother had called him seeking help with my depressed state.

At any rate, he visited with me for some time and asked me one question: Did I still want to be a priest—not a missionary but perhaps a diocesan priest, working in a diocese in the States? I said that I wasn't sure and that perhaps the right thing for me to do was to enter the service and serve my time. Then when I came out, I could decide the answer to his question. He told me that he believed I'd never go on to the priesthood after my time in the service. It was now or never, and if I decided I wanted to go on, he'd help find a diocese that would accept me.

I told him that I'd think it over and get back to him in a few weeks. He cautioned me not to wait too long because once my draft number came up, it would be increasingly difficult to keep out of the draft. After discussing it with my family and a few close friends, I decided to follow the priest's advice. I really did want to be a priest and truly believed that I had a calling to that vocation.

That same priest talked to the local draft board and made some calls to bishops around the country. Bishop John P. Treacy, a native of Boston but now the bishop of the La Crosse Diocese in Wisconsin, showed an interest. He was trying to recruit candidates who would serve in that diocese. He was in Boston at that time and agreed to meet with me. I wasn't overly optimistic, but the bishop apparently felt that I'd be a suitable candidate and accepted me, based on the older priest's strong recommendation.

So, without a break in my academic studies, I left in September of 1953 for Milwaukee, Wisconsin. I enrolled at St. Francis Major Seminary, on the banks of Lake Michigan, and started my second year of theology in new surroundings, with new classmates, and in a very different culture.

I found St. Francis to be much more structured and the rules stricter than at Maryknoll, but I was warmly welcomed by most members of my class and soon felt right at home. My years spent at St. Francis were uneventful. The longer I stayed, the more I realized that it had probably been for the best that I had switched from missionary to diocesan status. I was more adaptable to working with my own countrymen and felt less pressure.

The years passed quickly and soon I was nearing the time of my ordination. During the summer after our third theology and ordination to the deaconate, the members of our class from the La Crosse diocese were expected to spend a portion of our summer working in local parishes. We were assigned by the pastors to visit homes and to take a census of the Catholics living there. For the most part, it was enjoyable.

It gave us a chance to see how well we could work with the laity and to get a taste of parochial life.

During my years at St. Francis, I volunteered to work with members of the laity who wanted a refresher course in Catholic doctrine. I was assigned to assist a middle-aged couple who had both been afflicted with a form of tuberculosis. (Both would later fully recover and return to an active life.) They invited me to have Thanksgiving dinner with them, and since I was too far from home to be with my mother, I accepted.

From that time on, I developed a deep friendship with that couple and they even came to my ordination. Both have long since passed away, but I still have fond memories of our relationship. Their kindness and their support of my efforts to reach the priesthood were the first real experience I had in working with the laity. It helped convince me that I'd found my true vocation and that I could truly be of service to others. Years later, when I was struggling with my decision to leave the clerical life, it was that unique kind of service to others I knew I'd miss the most.

Chapter Three
To Serve God and His People

My Ordination, May 19th, 1956

On May 19, 1956, I was ordained a priest in the Cathedral of the Holy Cross in La Crosse, Wisconsin. Bishop John Treacy presided, and to this day I still remember his admonition to us after ordination. In fact, I remember that more than having made a promise to remain celibate. I guess I was so brainwashed that I just took the celibacy requirement in stride.

What I remembered most was his requiring us to make an added promise that we wouldn't take any alcohol for five years. He said it was to protect us from people who would encourage us to "just have a drink, Father, to celebrate our marriage, birthday, or whatever" and perhaps get ourselves into serious trouble or even become alcoholics. (I learned many years later that I was the only one who took him seriously.) One of my colleagues, trying to test the bishop, asked if that even applied to beer.

The bishop's answer was, "Beer also!"

Although my parents were separated, they both came to my ordination, as did my brother and his wife and two very close friends from Boston and Milwaukee. On the way home to Boston, I had arranged with someone at the Maryknoll seminary in New York to let me stay overnight so I could visit my classmates who were all on retreat, preparing for their own ordination a week later.

From left to right: Marie, brother George, Jim, father George

I arranged to offer my first Mass on their behalf. That was a very moving experience. There I was, celebrating the Eucharist for those I'd been forced to leave three year earlier. It's interesting how God works things out in our lives—often for the better.

My mother, especially, was on Cloud Nine. How she had waited for that day! It probably made up for a great amount of suffering she had experienced with my father leaving her for someone else and for my brother leaving the active Faith. She was putting a lot on me to make things right. At least at that moment, she was wonderfully happy and proud to say her son was a priest. (Sad to say, she was in for more suffering toward the end of her life.)

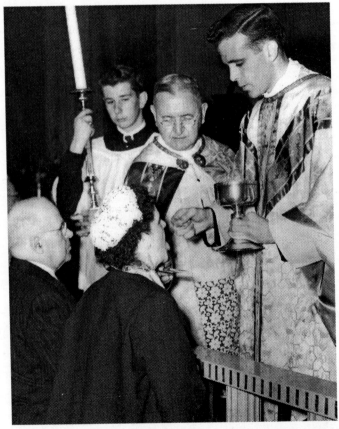

Serving Eucharist to Mother (Marie) at my first mass

Many of our relatives and close friends were present for my First Solemn Mass at my mother's parish, St. Mary's, in Lynn, Massachusetts. Three close priest friends who had helped me along the way to the priesthood attended me. Those were glorious days of innocence. I truly believed that my happiness was complete. I was surprised and pleased when some of my high school classmates held a party for me at one of their homes. Some were Catholic, but most weren't, yet they all seemed to feel a sense of pride in my accomplishment.

One experience during my home stay remains deeply embedded in my consciousness. It happened the Saturday night before I was to

return to Wisconsin for my first parish assignment. The pastor of St. Mary's, Msgr. McGlinchey, called me at my mother's home, asking me to take his confessional that night, since he had to be out of town. (Remember that it was the mid-50s, when most Catholics still went to private confession very frequently.)

First Solemn Mass 1956, St. Mary's Church, Lynn, Massachusetts

I was very nervous and felt completely unprepared. I made a mild protest, saying that I didn't yet have "faculties" to hear confession, not until I returned to La Crosse. The good pastor was unimpressed.

He hesitated a moment and then said, in a stern, husky voice, "Well, you have them now!"

That ended the conversation. I heard confessions that night for three straight hours and came out of the confessional in a deep sweat. When some of the other assistant pastors saw me, they good naturedly asked me how I did. I was speechless. What a lesson in humility! I really believe that it was at that moment when I first realized how little my seminary training had done to prepare me for interaction with the laity. The hundred or more confessions I heard that night weren't made by "bad" people. They were just troubled, caring people who were looking for the strength (not condemnation) to keep striving to be better singles, parents, students, workers, neighbors, and family members. For me, it was both a revelation and an inspiration. I was suddenly conscious of my unworthiness to be hearing their confessions, and I still had much to prove about myself and my capacity to love and truly forgive.

I will never forget a little incident that happened while a priest friend was driving me to Logan Airport in Boston for my flight back to Wisconsin and the beginning of my ministry. Like many Massachusetts drivers, we had someone following us who showed his impatience by sounding his horn several times, but Father just ignored him. Then the funniest thing happened. The driver found an opportunity to pass us and as he roared past on Father's side, we looked over and smiled. The driver was just beginning to form harsh words of contempt when he caught sight of Father's collar. Being the "good " Italian Catholic that he was, his mouth dropped and the yell his lips had formed suddenly dissolved into a meek greeting of "G—good morning, Father." Once he had passed us, we both roared with laughter at the transformation.

Of course, that was a typical reaction of any Catholic in those days when confronted with such a surprise. It told a lot about the reverence in which priests were held in that period of time. I wonder what he would have said today!

I don't remember much about my trip to Eau Claire, Wisconsin. My first parish assignment was as assistant pastor to the founder and pastor of Immaculate Conception Church. Everything was new. The church had just recently been completed. The same was true of the rectory and the parish school.

The taxi from the local airport left me off at the rectory. As I headed up the walk, I was impressed with the magnificence of the buildings. All of them were made of Lannon stone and brick. As I glanced around the neighborhood, I saw an array of well built homes and well kept grounds.

This was certainly not an inner city parish. These people had sacrificed much to pay for such an imposing group of church buildings.

The pastor wasn't at home to greet his new curate. Instead, there was a note advising me to go next door to the school and ask for the Sister Principal. She was expecting me and would have a key to let me into the rectory. I found her to be a very fine and friendly person. I believe that there were eight nuns in all, and they all made me feel right at home.

I was amazed and somewhat embarrassed to learn at a later time about their quarters. They had one large classroom with simple curtains as dividers for bedrooms. I hadn't yet seen my quarters next door in the rectory, but once I did, I was all the more shocked to realize the contrast in our accommodations. However, in those days, no one seemed surprised and simply accepted it, because nothing was too good for the "wonderful Fathers."

I had just enough time to bring my luggage in when the pastor arrived home. He apologized for not being at the rectory to meet me, but he'd had pressing business elsewhere. No sooner had we met than in came Fr. 'Mac', a huge man, a former Jesuit, much older than I, who had just transferred to the La Crosse diocese. He would live at the rectory and help out with Masses and the other Sacraments, but was assigned to teach at the Catholic high school, Regis, which was located in our parish, less than a mile away.

The pastor gave us a tour of the rectory, a huge living room (which we rarely used, except for times when he wanted to talk to us after lunch). Our evening meals were on our own, since we didn't initially have a housekeeper or cook. There were three ample offices, one for each of us, to meet with parishioners. The kitchen and dining room were also large but, as I recall, quite sterile.

Then he showed us the second floor apartments. His apartment was very large. Ours were smaller, but still very suitable, considering the space the nuns had next door, and also because we'd just come from the seminary, where living space was tight, to say the least. Each of us had a living room/study, a bedroom, and a private bath. I felt as if we were living in luxury.

After our tour had ended, Fr. Mac, as we called him, made a statement that echoed in my thoughts, but it was the pastor's response that gave me the first clue that it wasn't going to be a relaxed atmosphere and there was trouble on the horizon.

Fr. Mac said, "Father, this is palatial."

The pastor was obviously taken aback by that. Was Fr. Mac calling it a castle?

He glared at Fr. Mac for just a second and then, with a coldness that should have frozen us all solid, he replied, "Very plain, Father, very plain!"

With that, the tour ended abruptly and the pastor said we'd be going out to eat shortly.

The pastor took us to the Crossroads Café, which we soon found was to be our regular evening dining experience. Naturally he didn't have dinner with us again. He went somewhere else, often to one of the parishioner's homes. I really didn't mind, because the food was very good and the helpings were plentiful. I did find out shortly that the pastor and priests at St. Patrick's parish on the other side of town always ate at the White House restaurant, the hangout for most of the priests in the area. (There were five parishes in Eau Claire: St. Olaf's, Sacred Heart, St. James the Greater, Immaculate Conception, and St. Patrick's.)

I'll never forget the night (months later) when relations with the pastor had deteriorated significantly (especially between Fr. Mac and the pastor). The arrangement we had with the pastor was to always eat at the café (to save money) and we were required to get a receipt so the pastor could see how much our meals were costing the parish. Fr. Mac decided to call the pastor's bluff, so he ordered the most expensive meal, a porterhouse steak with all the fixings and a huge dessert. I was envious, but didn't want to upset the pastor, so I just ordered the usual.

When we arrived back at the rectory, Fr. Mac left the receipt taped to the pastor's door. The pastor never said one word about it, but I knew he was furious—and that Fr. Mac's days were numbered. Other arrangements would soon be made for his quarters.

The people at Immaculate Conception parish were wonderful and I soon had many invitations to dinner. However, the pastor always found reasons why a particular date was unsuitable. He made sure I had certain parish duties to attend to so I'd have to decline all invitations. I guess he didn't like any competition, but he let me know in no uncertain terms that I shouldn't be dining at any homes in the parish. It might cause scandal and embarrassment to those who felt as if they should also be extending an invitation but couldn't afford to. Of course, that rule didn't apply to him. After all, he was the *pastor* and father of the flock!

My work in the parish was quite diversified. I was assigned to visit the grade school classrooms to "talk about religion." The nuns were very tolerant of that, even though I suspected that they had a much better grasp of religious subjects and how to communicate with students in grades one through eight than I did. My coming in was only a formality so children could learn great wisdom from the new curate who was still wet behind the ears and about as relevant as a medieval knight! I was also expected to work with the boys sports teams and their coaches.

Finally, I was the spiritual father to adult groups meeting in the church hall. Those were my extracurricular duties in addition to offering weekday and Sunday Masses. (We didn't do Saturday afternoon Masses until after Vatican II.) I had a few baptisms and marriages, but only when the pastor had to be away. (Marriages and baptisms brought some pretty hefty stipends).

In those 50s days, parishioners still frequented the confessional box on a weekly (or at least monthly) basis, so all three of us were required to be present on Saturday afternoons and evenings for the many hours of absolving sinners. Frankly, I found very few people who really needed absolution. Perhaps that was why such inane penances as "three Our Fathers and three Hail Mary's" were so prevalent.

One of my favorite responsibilities was to visit the sick in the hospital and in their homes. It was most rewarding, since very often the elderly patients received very few visitors and many of them were somewhat fearful of their end days. They needed cheering up and encouragement to dwell on all the good moments of their lives and how they had helped others just by their presence in those people's lives.

I recall two people who remain vivid in my mind, almost fifty years later. One was an elderly woman who lived alone and was very poor. She wasn't well educated but had an abundance of common sense. Her attitude and friendship helped me get through some self-pity that I detected in myself. Her only son was a cross-country truck driver, and he was her only other visitor besides myself. He didn't visit often, but she really looked forward to his few visits. (Actually, I never met him.)

A couple of years after I left the parish and was taken up with other duties that absorbed much of my time, I learned that she had died—alone. I felt guilty that I hadn't continued to visit her. My only consolation was that she had finished her struggles and was now with God—I was sure of that!

The other parishioner at Immaculate Conception I recall was a young woman, probably in her early twenties. She was bedridden and an invalid. Her head was normal size, but her mother told me that the rest of her withered body was without feeling. It's interesting that I remember both her first name and that of the elderly woman I just mentioned—they were both called Mary. The invalid Mary was super-intelligent and read voraciously. She never complained about her infirmity and told me of her great plans to become a lawyer. She had already finished high school and was well along with her college studies. Her parents told me that Mary had already lived beyond medical expectations and that her end could come at any moment.

A short time later, Mary died peacefully. I can't remember if I visited her shortly before her death or whether, like the other Mary,

I was only told of her passing, but I'm sure that both Marys have a special place in heaven.

While my year at Immaculate Conception parish was a good one and I enjoyed all of the work I was assigned, my relationship with the pastor went downhill rapidly. As expected, Fr. Mac didn't last six months. His relationship with the pastor was a disaster. They were two stubborn Irishmen who were never meant to live under the same roof for long.

I remember with amusement the incident that pushed the pastor over the precipice. He never liked the arrangement with Mac, which consisted of Mac's teaching at Regis and spending every waking moment at the school. Mac really considered Fr. John Rossiter, an outwardly tough, yet fun-loving principal, as his true—and only—boss.

The pastor took much pleasure in giving Fr. Mac early Sunday morning Masses and in the fact that Fr. Mac had great difficulty getting up early after late evening sessions with other faculty members. Fr. Mac eventually discovered a way to get back at the pastor—and unintentionally at me, as well. He came home one day and showed me a huge alarm clock he had purchased. Then he told me his plan and swore me to secrecy. I must admit that I was a willing accomplice.

The following Sunday morning (at approximately 5:30 am), I was awakened by the most god-awful sound I'd ever heard. Mac had set the alarm and placed it in the tub in his bathroom (with all the doors left ajar). It sounded like the loudest fire alarm you could imagine—and he let it ring for almost five minutes before turning it off.

The war had reached a crescendo, and inside of a week's time, Fr. Mac had his wish—the pastor had arranged for his exile. You've never seen such a happy and relieved priest as Fr. Mac as he swiftly packed his belongings and bid us all a fond farewell. (Little did I know then that I'd also be gone from the parish within nine months.)

With Fr. Mac out of the way, the pastor turned on me as his next victim. During the first few months of my tenure, I'd been able to do no wrong and the pastor praised me to all the parishioners as the ideal curate. But suddenly, he changed his mind and I could do no right! Life became intolerable and it took a lot of willpower not to complain about him to some of my closest friends in the parish.

I soon realized that the pastor had an underground network of spies who reported my every move. He'd ask me to come into the living room after lunch and then he'd tell me all of the terrible things I was doing to turn the parish against him. I objected, but in those days the role of curate was lower than the housekeeper the pastor finally hired or the men who took care of the grounds. I was a non-person, and if I complained to the chancery or other priests, I was labeled a troublemaker.

CHAPTER FOUR
A BLESSING OF SORTS

It was about then that a miracle happened. Fr. John Rossiter came to my rescue with an offer I couldn't refuse. He'd been assigned by the bishop to serve as chaplain, along with his other duties, to the students and faculty at Wisconsin State University in Eau Claire (a branch of the University of Wisconsin, Madison.), and he soon realized that he couldn't give adequate time to that venture without neglecting his primary duties as principal of Regis High School. So he came to me with an offer to take his place as Newman chaplain as a part-time responsibility. I said I'd be delighted, but I knew the pastor would be furious.

John said, "Don't worry about it. Bishop Treacy and I are good friends and I'll simply ask him to make the announcement."

Inside of two weeks, I'd been named John's replacement. The pastor was furious and made his feelings known to the bishop. He used every argument in the book to have the bishop recant, but Bishop Treacy (God bless him) stood firm and I never heard another peep out of the pastor. Little did he (or I, for that matter) know what was to transpire in a few months' time.

Fr. Rossiter introduced me to the officers of the Newman Club at their next meeting and told them that I'd be taking over as part-time chaplain. I started in with great enthusiasm and began planning activities with the officers. The pastor kept putting stone blocks in my way by telling me that I needed to consult with him before attending Newman meetings and getting too involved with Catholics on the

State campus, and I did the best I could to serve two masters, but it became increasingly frustrating to have my efforts blocked over and over again. So, after a few months, I talked to John Rossiter and asked his advice on what measures I should take to resolve my dilemma.

John told me to write the bishop and explain how difficult it was to do justice to both the campus ministry and to the demands of the pastor, which I did immediately. I received a call from the Chancellor of the diocese, asking me to come to La Crosse to meet with him and Bishop Treacy. I made an appointment and drove to the bishop's residence next to the seminary. The bishop was very understanding and said he wanted me to be able to give my undivided attention to the campus ministry.

After the meeting, the Chancellor told me to call him in about a week. I called him exactly one week from the meeting and he told me that Bishop Treacy had decided to make my appointment fulltime. As soon as I could find a suitable building for my living accommodations, office space, and a room to hold Mass, he'd make the announcement and the diocese would proceed with the purchase of the first Newman Center on the Eau Claire State campus.

I was ecstatic. Much as I hated to leave the people at Immaculate Conception parish, I knew that it was an opportunity to be out on my own, filling a very important apostolate. (Of course, it was also an opportunity to be out from under the iron fist of the pastor!)

It didn't take long to find a house for sale near the campus. I met with a realtor and provided the diocese with all of the particulars. A diocesan representative came to Eau Claire from La Crosse and within a few weeks we were ready to move in. I purchased the few necessities I'd need and announced to the pastor that I'd be moving out. He'd anticipated that and had already asked for an assistant to replace me.

The new assistant, also a native of Boston, was a wonderful priest, a few years older than I. He and the pastor seemed to hit it off very well and he stayed on as his assistant for many years. As I recall, when the pastor was finally transferred, the assistant was named the new pastor. So, it all worked out for the best.

As a footnote, I need to mention that the likeable principal of Regis High School, Fr. John Rossiter, met a tragic end to his ministry some years later when he was the pastor of a La Crosse parish. He was shot to death by a mentally deranged parishioner while Fr. Rossiter was at the altar, offering Mass. John's brother, Richard, who was also a high school principal and priest, later died prematurely of cancer. It was a tragic loss to a wonderful family.

I spent the next 14 years as a Newman chaplain, with only a one-and-a-half-year sabbatical to study for a doctorate in ecumenical theology at St. Rose Dominican Priory in Dubuque, Iowa (1967–68). I'll get to that in due time. I was appointed chaplain in 1957, scarcely a year after my ordination in May 1956. I found the work stimulating, but not without some setbacks and frustrations. I was still an "old school" priest, and Vatican II was still six years in the future.

We offered Mass in Latin with no participation from the laity except for a server who answered our prayers—in Latin—and I faced the wall with my back to the people. On Sundays and Holy Days, as well as Ash Wednesday and Blessing of Throats in February, we packed the living room, chapel, and the front doorway with students attending Mass. On weekdays, there were only a few of the more devout Catholics who came regularly.

One of those, Jerry Harpt, from Marinette, Wisconsin, always served Mass when he could come. (Jerry and I have remained friends more than four decades and my wife, Jackie, and I visit Jerry and his wife, Karen, whenever we get to Jackie's home state.)

I served as chaplain to the Knights of Columbus and they sponsored a rosary program at the center for years. We worked out a plan with Jack Kelly, one of the managers of the local radio station (TV was still in its infancy) to broadcast the rosary for shut-ins. That continued for several years and attracted both students and townspeople.

Father Jim and Jerry Harpt (former college altar boy, lifelong friend) 1960

One of my most embarrassing events, which happened early on in my student ministry, was an indicator of how far to the right I was regarding church practice. While a good number of students took advantage of the Newman community on campus, I was somewhat disturbed that so many seemed indifferent. I shared my feelings with some of the students and may have even brought it up at our monthly meetings. However, it had little or no impact on most people. I even thought of writing a letter to the parents, but I took a more drastic approach—and paid a severe price.

I composed a letter to all Catholic students on campus and after much soul searching, I sent it out. I never dreamed it would get the response it did. As I recall, I threatened to refuse Communion to those who didn't join and participate in the Newman program on campus.

I was away when the letter was received, but on my return, a handful of my loyal students came to let me know the mood of the student body. They were calling for an emergency meeting the next day. They suggested that I let them handle the meeting and at an appropriate time, I could address those present. I was stunned. What had I done, except to defend the church's insistence that they practice their faith?

We held the meeting on campus and it was the largest turnout of Catholic students and faculty I had ever witnessed. It was soon obvious that they were out to have my scalp. One after another, they castigated me for my sending such a letter. Some of them demanded to know whether I had the right or authority to make such demands of students attending a secular university. I was humiliated, as I should have been. However, it was an extreme example of how a well intentioned product of the seminary of the 1950s could misinterpret the spirit of the Gospel.

I was way out of line and the only reason I kept my position as chaplain was due to the magnanimous intervention of the president of the college, Leonard Haas, a good friend and a popular personage on campus. He had been informed of the letter and its impact on Catholic students, and defended my right to say what I had, but admitted that it was undoubtedly done in haste and gave me a chance to explain. The diocese was also informed and while they defended me, they mildly reprimanded me for taking such an unprecedented stand.

Bishop Treacy dedicated our chapel at the Newman Center in 1957. We had an outdoor Mass on the grounds of the center and a large turnout of Catholic students and faculty were on hand to help us celebrate.

Shortly after the dedication, a friend of the bishop, Msgr. P.J. O'Connor, invited me to join him on a flight to Miami, Florida, to attend the installation of Bishop Coleman Carroll, the first named bishop of the new diocese. Until that time, the Diocese of St. Augustine was the only Catholic diocese in that state. (Now, almost fifty years later, there are at least eight dioceses, reflecting the tremendous growth in Florida's Catholic population.)

Bishop Treacy gladly approved of my accepting P.J.'s invitation, so I flew out of Milwaukee and joined the Monsignor in Atlanta (where he was pastor of Immaculate Conception Shrine Church). It was quite a treat for a young, newly ordained priest.

We attended the Mass Installation in the cathedral and then drove to Edon Roc Hotel on Miami Beach, where the dinner celebration drew bishops and priests from all forty-eight and beyond. I believe that the apostolic delegate representing the ailing Pope Pius XII was also in attendance. I was in awe to see all the giants of the church assembled at the head table, including Cardinal Cushing of Boston, Cardinal Spellman of New York, and Spellman's arch rival, Bishop Fulton J. Sheen, a media star with a weekly television show.

A humorous thing took place during the dinner. Bishop Sheen was late, so he made a grand entrance that drew the attention of hundreds of reporters covering the event and sustained applause from the enormous audience. That didn't sit well with Cardinal Spellman, but he overlooked it. However, what followed made him visibly sick and one could see his heightened agitation.

Halfway through the dinner, there was an interruption. A public address announcement requested Bishop Sheen to come to the lobby for a phone call from India. It had been staged, but who could object, since Sheen held the position of National Prefect for the Propagation of the Faith? A broad smile covered his face as Sheen made a regal exit from the room full of dignitaries.

Pope Pius XII died while we were in Florida. Eugeneio Pacelli had been a product of Italian aristocracy and a staunch supporter of the status quo in both church doctrine and practice. He'd been pope for as long as I could remember and his passing created mixed emotions. He wasn't really known by the laity or most of the clergy. We thought of him as an imposing figure who appeared weekly above the crowds gathered in Vatican City to give them his blessing—in Latin—and then disappeared again into the shadows.

He almost never traveled outside of Rome, and I don't recall him ever traveling to the United States, at least during his pontificate. As was usual when a pope died, there was much speculation about his successor. We expected the new pope to be another Italian. We also believed that the new pope would be much like, if not a clone of, Pius XII. So you can imagine our surprise when the College of Cardinals elected a very old man as his successor. It was rumored that it had been done because they wanted an interim pope to serve for a few years and then be succeeded by someone younger and more vigorous to carry on Pius the XII's lengthy pontificate.

Contrary to the designs of the Curia (the ruling cardinals in Rome) Roncalli was anything but a stand-in for the next pope. Pope John XXIII would make his mark on the papacy in such a remarkable way that few people could have imagined. A hint to what he had in mind came in the first month of his pontificate, when he told a close ally that he intended to "open the dusty windows of the Vatican and allow both light and clean air to permeate the place." (That may be a loose translation of his words, but it conveys the essence of what he said.)

John XXIII was no interim pope. He was only to live for the next five years, but in that time he turned the Catholic Church on its head. Almost immediately, against strong resistance from his advisors, he set in motion the plans for the first worldwide Church Council since Vatican I, almost a century before (1870). He made it clear that he wanted the council to take place during his pontificate and set 1962 as the date for the first session.

Vatican II lasted three years. John opened its first session and forever left his stamp on its proceedings. Unfortunately for the world, he wasn't to see its conclusion. He died prematurely during the second session, but during his all-too-brief tenure in office, we all grew to love that octogenarian whose appearance belied what was within.

He was a homely man and much too stout, but when he smiled, the world smiled with him. He was kind and loving and had a great sense of humor. He wore the robes of office humbly and without the affectation of his predecessors. It was soon obvious to all who witnessed his words and his actions that while he didn't want to be called His Holiness, he truly was a holy man. He unabashedly loved people—all people—and he understood the needs and concerns of those who looked to him for spiritual guidance.

I believe that was the most Christ-like pope who ever sat in the Chair of Peter. We all had great hopes for the church in those days of Reformation. Some of us even hoped that the church, under his leadership, would restore the 1000-year tradition of a married clergy—but to no avail!

A number of events were responsible for my conversion from a conservative, unquestioning cleric to a more liberal, and might I say more human, follower of Christ—the Christ I'd come to see in the faces and hearts of the people I served. One of those events took place while I was in Eau Claire, at the height of the Vietnam War—in 1966 or 1967.

At that time, support for the struggle was still at fever pitch among most Americans, and I was one of them. Then one night, I was at a student meeting when a newly returned veteran was being questioned about his experience. He let it be known that he wasn't proud of what was going on in Vietnam. He told of his experience as a member of a helicopter crew and how they questioned Vietcong prisoners.

They'd take several prisoners up in the helicopter and start questioning them. If they didn't get the information they wanted, they'd throw one of them out—to certain death. Then they'd turn to the next one and repeat the same process. At the time, he justified the practice because of what he'd seen done to his comrades. But at that meeting, far removed from that hellish experience, he was no longer sure and was doomed to nightmares that he found hard to live with.

For the first time, I began to have doubts about our engagement in Vietnam.

My own convictions were put to the test a year or so later. There was a group on campus that belonged to a national protest group called Students for a Democratic Society (SDS). Their sole intent was to convince the U.S. government to end the war in Vietnam. On one occasion, they planned a massive demonstration on campus against the war. They had invited a Quaker professor whose pacifist beliefs were well known on campus to speak against the war on the steps of the post office, which also housed an office of the FBI.

I had great respect for Dr. Lutz, but I wasn't yet ready to make my own position public. The SDS organizers wanted a campus minister to say a prayer on the steps prior to Dr. Lutz's remarks. They had approached a Methodist minister and a Lutheran minister, but both of them were going to be out of town, so they came to me and asked if I'd be willing to say the prayer. They promised the demonstration would be peaceful. They only intended to have their followers walk through town with signs and to end up on the steps of the post office. I told them I'd think about it and give them my answer the next day.

Deep down, I wished they didn't ask me. My brother had served during WWII and my father had been in both world wars and had just retired. I prayed hard for direction and tried to rationalize myself out of it. The students came back the next morning for my answer, and I told them I'd do it.

Then came the tough part. I marched with the group, wearing my collar. I'd been in town for quite a few years and most people knew me. The hardest part was passing a group of veterans (from a number of wars). They booed Dr. Lutz by name, but they said nothing to me. On the steps of the post office, I prayed that we'd end the war, which was dividing the nation like no other conflict we'd been associated with.

The next day, the local paper criticized us for being disloyal to America—and even called us traitors. One Catholic man that I knew wrote a letter to the editor in which he really took me to task. He said that I shouldn't have worn a black cassock (which I didn't—I'd been dressed in street clothes, but he wanted to make a point). He said I should have worn a red cassock. I guess he was implying that I was a communist!

Those were difficult times. In light of history, I'm glad now that I marched. It took me off the fence and made me realize that many times we must espouse unpopular causes when we truly believe that it's the right thing to do. That was a critical moment in my political—and probably spiritual—conversion.

On a lighter note, I spearheaded a program to raise money for the Newman organization. I met with a group of laypeople who were also interested in supporting us. I don't remember how we contacted our first celebrity guest performer, but we invited Jack Haley, Sr. (who played the part of the Tin Man in the 1939 production of *The Wizard of Oz*). We heard that he was a Catholic and a great after-dinner speaker.

He agreed to come, so we started the first of a series of fundraising dinners. In 1960 we invited the Lennon Sisters, the vocal quartet on the *Lawrence Welk Show*. The next year, it was Dennis Day, a tenor singer on the *Jack Benny Show*. We also had the Little Gaelic Singers from Dublin, Ireland, and finally, Bob Newhart, who was just getting his start as a comedian.

Not only did the dinners bring in some much-needed money, but they also involved a large number of students who wouldn't otherwise have shown much interest. They also brought a fun, exciting atmosphere that welcomed students to find out more about the Newman Center and the Catholic faith without demanding immediate involvement in the church.

For the most part, those were happy years, and I learned a great deal about life while working with those young people during the most formative years of their lives.

CHAPTER FIVE
ALWAYS SEARCHING AND PRAYING

One of the most wonderful assignments I received as a priest was that of administrator of a small country parish approximately fifteen miles from Eau Claire while still maintaining my chaplaincy to students at the local university. It was a welcome addition to my primary responsibilities and gave me an opportunity to serve a community, mostly on the weekends, when many of the students were at home.

St. Bridget's served a small farming community of about 100 families. The people were wonderful and extremely delighted that they now had their own pastor. I spent a good part of each weekend at the parish, celebrating Mass and hearing confessions, as well as baptizing the newborn. Most weeks, I also went out for one evening of meetings or when I was called to minister. I couldn't have been happier in my dual role and never considered myself overworked. I even had a little black-and-white terrier who would ride with me in the car out into the country. What a picture we made—me in my black suit and Roman collar, and Blackie in the front seat next to me.

Imagine my disappointment when the chancellor called me one night (after I'd been serving the parish for about a year and a half) and told me that the bishop was relieving me of that responsibility, not because of any infractions on my part, but because the diocese had an older priest with alcohol abuse problems and they were trying to find a place for him to serve where he could do the least amount of harm. I thought it was an insult to those good people and a disservice to me.

Then, to add insult to injury, they told me they were sending him to live with me at the Newman Center.

We had moved the center to a new location next to the campus. That home was much larger and had ample space for another priest, and though I had no objection to sharing the facility, removing me from that parish without consulting me and then sending my replacement to live with me seemed to be a very insensitive decision. However, that's the way the church operated forty years ago—and still does!

I was crushed by the action, but what could I do? It was an example of how the church protected its offending priests at the expense of those who were trying to do their best to serve with integrity. It was also one of the experiences that caused me to question whether or not I could live a totally celibate life until my death. I felt the loneliness of not having someone in whom I could confide and I received little compassion from other priests in the area.

I was aware of the injustices that existed in the business world, where people often betrayed or put others down in order to establish a more lucrative or powerful position for themselves, but I was still quite naïve when it came to political machinations within the church. I always believed that if you did a good job in one assignment, you deserved every consideration for future promotions.

In the ensuing years, I watched good men (who were also excellent priests) sacrificed by the institution if it seemed to be for the good of the church. I found that the bishop had his favorites—men who were totally loyal to him and the church and never questioned his decisions. That attitude, I believe, is what led to the secrecy among the clergy in defending actions that should have been denounced. If we had more priests willing to expose what we've experienced in the past few years, I believe we'd have a more purified church and a laity with greater faith and confidence in its leaders—and the pedophile epidemic probably would have been discovered and halted ten, twenty, or even thirty years ago.

I was nearing my tenth year in the priesthood and felt that I needed some kind of sabbatical. I needed a temporary change from my Newman work, so I requested a new assignment from our new bishop (Bishop Treacy had died shortly after the end of the Vatican II Council). He offered me three choices. The first was to enter the military chaplaincy. That interested me, and I made some inquiries, but because of my age (late 30s), I'd only be eligible to enter the army's program, in which clergymen up to the age of 40 could apply. However, before I could take my first step in that direction, the bishop informed me that the option had been taken off the table. He decided that he had enough chaplains in military posts.

His second offer was to replace one of our La Crosse priests at a mission we administered in South America. That appealed to me, but I insisted that I needed time to study the language before being shipped out. I felt it was only fair to the people (and to me), but the bishop couldn't wait. He wanted an immediate replacement.

That left me with his third offer—to go on for graduate studies in theology. I decided that offer made the most sense, so I requested that I be allowed to study for a doctorate in Ecumenical Studies at the Dominican Priory in Dubuque, Iowa. The bishop gave his approval, and I took an eighteen-month leave of absence to enter graduate school. Not only were the studies ecumenical, but the faculty and students were from various denominations.

I found the program exciting and challenging. It was another opportunity to grow spiritually and intellectually. During my ten years of seminary study, I had been in a totally Catholic environment. That period of my life had opened me to ideas and beliefs that I'd never encountered before.

During my time at St. Rose Priory, I developed a deep respect for the Dominican priests and brothers and formed some close friendships. In fact, toward the end of my studies there, I was invited by several Dominicans to accompany them on a trip to Washington, D.C., in 1968. The Vietnam War was at its height and opposition to the war was growing in the United States. We participated in a march on Washington, which included many notable opponents, the best known among them being Dr. Martin Luther King, leader of the Civil Rights Movement and an outspoken critic of our involvement in Vietnam.

While in Washington, we visited a number of congressmen and tried to enlist their support for the campaign to end the war. Some were very supportive, others argumentative in support of the administration, and a few openly hostile to our presence. It was an issue that was dividing our nation (much like the war in Iraq is dividing us today).

Toward the end of our stay, a march had been planned to Arlington National Cemetery, where a nonviolent protest would be led by Dr. King. I was torn between participating or refraining from that march. I really wanted to be part of it, but I feared that my father, who was still living at that time, might see me on television, and I couldn't bring myself to hurt him when he was so ill. He was a veteran of two world wars and the Korean conflict and he supported our presence in Vietnam. Perhaps my actions were inexcusable—and perhaps even cowardly—but I had to make a choice, and I made it, in deference to him.

I had completed all of the course work and had passed all my exams for the doctorate, with the exception of completing my dissertation. I probably made a mistake in returning to the diocese early with thoughts of finishing my thesis on religious freedom while taking up my new assignment as Newman chaplain at Wisconsin State University in Stevens Point, Wisconsin. As it turned out, I never completed the dissertation and never earned my degree. Other events in my life intervened!

I applied for and received a Danforth grant to do research on my dissertation in Europe. It was to be my second trip abroad. (Earlier in my priesthood, I had taken a chaplaincy on an oceanic trip during Holy Week to several ports, including Ireland, England, France, and Germany.) I served as Catholic chaplain on the *USS America* (a reconverted troop ship during World War II).

We traveled out of New York harbor and past the Statue of Liberty. It was quite an adventure for a youngster from Saugus, Massachusetts. My only other trip to New York had been in 1939, when I traveled with my family in my father's huge 1927 Pierce Arrow to take in the New York World's Fair, to see Johnny Weissmuller, the greatest swimmer of that time, and to enjoy a Broadway newcomer, Edgar Bergen and his talking dummy, Charlie McCarthy.

My 1963 trip to Europe was during the second session of the Vatican II Council. The changes to come in the Catholic Church were still in the discussion stage, so as a young priest, I was hardly aware of their consequences. My responsibilities on the ship were to offer daily Mass and be available for the needs of Catholics on board.

I remember well the Irish steward who cared for my cabin. He was probably a man in his 60s, and seemed pleased that he was to attend to the needs of an American Catholic priest. I soon learned that he had served as steward many years ago to President Kennedy's family when they sailed for England with the new ambassador, Joseph Kennedy, Sr. Little did we know then that before the year was out, the young president would be cut down by an assassin's bullets in Dallas!

One incident that sticks in my memory was the day I went swimming in the ship's pool and lingered after the other passengers had left. I was alone in the pool when we must have run into a squall and the ship began to rock. I tried desperately for several agonizing moments to reach the side of the pool but kept being swept backward with each movement of the ship. Fortunately, we finally leveled off and I was able to reach the safety of the side rail. All I could think of was how stupid it would sound if the newspapers carried a story of a priest chaplain drowning in the ship's pool. Needless to say, I was careful from then on to swim only when there were other passengers in the pool.

I was supposed to stay on board the ship at all times, even when we were in port, but my steward told me he'd get a message to the captain that I'd like to get off at Le Havre to take the boat train up to Paris, rather than going on to Bremerhaven, Germany. I was surprised when the captain consented, but I was warned that I had to be back to the docks at a set time when the ship was making its return trip.

I traveled to Paris for two days. (I had to return by Thursday to conduct services for the remaining days of Holy Week.) I enjoyed my two days on land immensely, staying at a little inn downtown. The highlight was attending Mass at the Basilica of the Sacred Heart (Sacre Coeur) and walking up the Champs Elysee to view the open air art markets that covered both sides of the cobblestone street.

On our return trip, I had the opportunity to visit the captain's bridge to see how the ship operated. We were told that the day we were on the bridge in early April 1963 was the anniversary date of the sinking of the Titanic in 1912. As we sailed over that very spot, we held a moment of silence in respect for the thousands of passengers who had perished on that cold night so many years before.

During my European trip in 1968, I missed the riots that took place in Detroit, Los Angeles, and Chicago during the '68 Democratic National Convention. I was in Europe from June 26th until September 3rd doing research on my doctoral thesis. With the help of a Danforth grant received at the end of my formal studies in Dubuque, I was able to fly to Europe and spend ten weeks in that pursuit.

I flew to Shannon Airport in Ireland and stayed for a few days with an Irish family, who were related to one of my childhood friends. I then flew to Paris, where I boarded one of Europe's finest trains and traveled for three days by coach across Western Europe and into the Scandinavian countries. My destination was Uppsala, Sweden, where I attended the World Council of Churches annual convention as a delegate.

My friend from Eau Claire State University, Dr. Howard Lutz, made arrangements with a friend of his who had an apartment in

Uppsala and was on vacation in the States, to let me use her apartment in her absence, saving me a great expense that I would otherwise have incurred. I found the meeting very useful, since it brought me into contact with many people whose knowledge and experience were invaluable to my research on the subject of religious liberty.

From there, I traveled back to Geneva, Switzerland, and then to Celigny, France, where I attended a three-week course in ecumenical theology involving students from all over the world. It was embarrassing to find out that most of the students were conversant in several languages, including English. There were only two other students from America besides myself, so we tended to stick together for support. One was a Lutheran minister and the other was an American Airlines pilot who had flown with Admiral Byrd on his last flight to Antarctica.

I have many memories of our studies in Celigny, but probably the most vivid is of an incident that took place shortly after the other two Americans and I had left and were staying overnight in Geneva. We learned of the Russian attack on Czechoslovakia and the deaths of many people. What really startled us, however, was the knowledge that three of the students at Celigny had left a few days earlier to return to their homeland—Czechoslovakia. We understandably feared for their safety.

I was in Tubingen, Germany, home of the famous theologian, Hans Kung, visiting a Jesuit House of Studies when we learned of Pope Paul VI's surprise encyclical, *Humanae Vitae*, in which he reasserted the Catholic Church's stand against artificial birth control—condemning its usage by all Catholics worldwide. The Jesuit scholars were furious. They reflected the mood of theologians everywhere and the impact it would have on millions of Catholics trying to abide by the Church's teachings while engaging in a struggle of conscience over its consequences. It was one more event that added to my doubts about continuing a life of celibacy.

The church seems to have no understanding of human conscience or extreme circumstances—everything is black and white, with no deviations. That mentality is driving throngs of Catholics out of the church. It did so in the late 60s and continues to accelerate—to the point that more people are leaving than coming in, and it's true of priests and those studying for the priesthood, as well.

Every layperson I speak with, whether they're no longer practicing their faith or are deeply-rooted "cradle Catholics," say the same thing: "When is the church going to wake up and realize that they're losing most educated Catholics who can no longer remain faithful to a hierarchical church that's so out of touch with the people?"

Using my Eurail Pass, I traveled all over Western Europe, visiting seventeen countries. What impressed me most was the number of young people I met on the trains and in the cities who were traveling from such exotic places as Japan, India, and even China. They added much to my education and my awareness of the world around me.

When I returned home, I was no longer assigned to the Newman Center in Eau Claire. My new assignment was to serve as chaplain to the students and faculty at Wisconsin State University in Stevens Point, and my assistant would be Fr. Joseph Sullivan. Fr. Joe should have been appointed senior chaplain, but he'd gotten into some trouble with the bishop.

It seems that Fr. Joe and Sister Margaret Elsen, SSND (who was also appointed to work with the chaplains) had attended the funeral of one of their colleagues, the Episcopal chaplain, and out of deference to him and his family, chose to receive Holy Communion with the others present at the funeral. Word leaked back to the bishop and he called both of them onto the carpet. He reprimanded them for giving "scandal to the faithful" (a common phrase of that era), and threatened to suspend Fr. Joe's faculties to offer Mass or to administer the sacraments.

He didn't trust Joe to be in charge of the center, so that's where I came in. Fresh back from graduate school and with ten years experience as Newman chaplain in Eau Claire, I was the likely candidate for such an assignment.

I learned a great deal from my shared responsibilities with Joe. I felt that he was a wonderful priest—and a wonderful human being. He helped me to move closer to the people and not to take myself so seriously. The students (and not just the Catholics) loved him and responded to him in ways they didn't respond to me. He was like a big brother to them and could have great fun with them while still retaining his priestly qualities. His Masses were something to behold, with lots of dialogue while still maintaining dignity.

I was fortunate to be able to work with him for almost three years. We lived in an apartment home near the campus and offered Mass for the students and faculty and others who preferred our Masses to those in the parish. We conducted services in the basement of St. Stanislaus Church.

As had been the case in Eau Claire, I met some wonderful people in Stevens Point. My wife and I still correspond with the Hoffmeisters, a wonderful couple who owned their own printing business in Stevens Point and from whom we receive an annual Christmas card, rich in humor and containing a picture of their growing family, which now numbers at least twenty, including children, spouses, and grandchildren. (A few years ago, we had a reunion with Dick and Lois while visiting Wisconsin.)

While the student parish and I fully appreciated Fr. Joe's gifts, the bishop and other clergy members weren't so enthusiastic. To them, Joe was simply a rebel and a troublemaker. I'll never forget an episode shortly before Fr. Joe was removed and suspended from his duties on the campus.

The bishop was coming to Stevens Point for some function and afterwards wanted to take me to dinner. I was somewhat flattered and my mother, who was visiting at the time, was thrilled to think that the bishop of the diocese was asking me to dinner. I did think it was strange, since he had never contacted me or visited during the two years I had been away at graduate school in Dubuque.

It wasn't long into the dinner that I fully realized why I had been so privileged. The bishop was out to get rid of Fr. Joe Sullivan and needed allies. He needed to hear from other priests who were critical of his actions. I'm sure that he'd already gotten ammunition from some of the pastors in the region, but he wanted to hear from me, since I was Joe's "superior." I was to pound the final nail in his coffin.

He asked me to describe Joe's activities. I was furious at the deception and the cruel way of damning a good priest. I looked him in the eye and told him that Fr. Joe Sullivan was a fine priest, well loved and respected by the students and townspeople who truly knew him. The bishop was visibly upset with my defense of Joe and quickly changed the subject. The dinner ended earlier than he had planned, but there was nothing more to talk about.

From that moment on, I lost whatever respect I'd had for the bishop. He was devious, calculating, and full of himself. I knew that I could never confide anything of worth with him ever again. That may help explain my decision not to visit him in advance of my plan to leave the clerical state a few years later.

That experience set in motion my decision to leave the clergy, although I wasn't ready to do it at that moment. I loved being a priest and most of the responsibilities I had as a priest. I enjoyed working with that age group. The students, for the most part, were honest about their feelings and convictions.

We were living in the 60s, a turbulent period in the latter part of the twentieth century. The Vietnam conflict, the assassination of President John F. Kennedy, the subsequent assassination of his brother, Robert, on the verge of capturing the 1968 Democratic nomination, and the assassination of Dr. Martin Luther King, Nobel Prize winner for promoting peace and leader of the National Civil Rights Movement, along with other significant events, had divided the nation and introduced a skepticism, especially in the young, that would reflect that period for decades to come.

CHAPTER SIX
SOMETHING IS MISSING

After my trip to Europe and my return to Wisconsin, I resumed my chaplaincy at Stevens Point. I had much to think about, not the least of which was my continuation in the priesthood. It seemed as if I heard of someone else who was leaving from the diocese almost every month and I wondered why the church was allowing the requirement of celibacy to stand as a stumbling block for so many good men who wanted to remain priests but were discovering the need to marry and have families.

During that time, I attended a special retreat with a number of other priests and laymen. It was called a *cursillo*. The concept had come to the United States from South America and was becoming very popular. It tried to help people in their daily lives and while rooted in faith, it also appealed to the heart and attempted to bring them into closer contact with their fellow men and women. My attendance at that retreat was to have a profound effect on the rest of my life, as will be evident in the pages to follow.

The retreat itself was excellent and I enjoyed the three-day weekend very much. There was always a priest moderator or leader, but the presentations were almost all given by laymen and laywomen from all walks of life, including housewives, businesspeople, educators, shopkeepers, physicians, engineers, and lawyers. Each one had a given topic, but they spoke out of their own life experience, which was what made their contributions so unique and valuable.

The cursillo made such an impression on me that I began formulating a plan to model that style of retreat for students and faculty back at the college. A few months after my introduction to that spiritual experience, I was asked by a priest classmate to assist him in giving a cursillo. I jumped at the opportunity to find out more.

We had a group of about thirty participants and all went well at first. Then my colleague gave a presentation on theology and I found myself at odds with him on a few particulars. I thought some of his interpretations were a little too liberal.

One of the nuns who was attending the cursillo with other members of her community began to side too much (I thought) with the other priest's ideas. A couple of times she challenged what I was saying and it began to aggravate me.

"Who does this woman think she is?" I thought. "Does she have a degree in theology?"

She was a member of the School Sisters of Notre Dame, a very strict order with a motherhouse in Milwaukee. I really began to dislike her. Surprisingly, we got along much better as time passed and the retreat went quite smoothly. In fact, I recall that at the end of the cursillo, some of the members thought I was a bit uptight, so they sang a special song, "Beautiful, Beautiful Brown Eyes," and dedicated it to me. I was very moved by that gesture and I became aware of that nun's fine voice—the same voice that had annoyed me during the first part of the retreat.

As we said our goodbyes at the end of the final day, that nun said that she'd like to talk to me about a decision she was trying to make. We talked for awhile and she told me that she had decided to leave the convent for personal reasons and would be leaving her teaching position in Chippewa Falls, Wisconsin. I don't remember the exact advice I gave her, but I admired her courage in leaving the community and returning to life as a layperson. While I said nothing about my own questioning of the clerical state, I believe that our conversation affected my own decision down the line.

Almost one year later, I was asked to lead a cursillo. At first I hesitated, but then I decided to accept the invitation. Again, we had some thirty participants, and the retreat went well. At the end of the last session, we had the traditional *ultrea*, which was a time for those who had attended past cursillos to come by and congratulate the newest participants. I was surprised to see Sr. Irenae (whose real name was Jackie Kresse) among that group, but it pleased me very much to see her again. Days later, I couldn't get Jackie out of my mind. I really wanted to see her again, but I didn't know how to arrange such a meeting, since she was still living at the convent in Chippewa Falls.

About a week after the cursillo, I had planned to drive from Stevens Point to Eau Claire to visit my mother, who was in the Sacred Heart Hospital. She was expecting me in the afternoon, so I called the convent and asked to speak to Sister Irenae. When she came to the phone, I explained that I was going to be visiting my mother in Eau Claire and wondered if she'd be interested in going to dinner afterward. I'm sure she was surprised, but she said that would be fine and we settled on a time for me to pick her up.

I should go back a few years and explain what had been going through my mind before saying more about our relationship. For a few years after Vatican II, I knew I still wanted to be a priest, but I was beginning to feel the loneliness of being single and without a family. I was also beginning to question my willingness to live a lifetime of celibacy.

I was almost forty and had truly lived a celibate life. I'd always been careful about any dealings with the opposite sex, even though my work as a Newman pastor brought me into contact with many young women, some of whom I found very attractive. However, I always kept them at a distance and was never alone with them, except in counseling sessions or when they came to confession.

At times I was even a little neurotic in that area, always fearful that I might cause a scandal. I even suggested that my mother ride in the backseat of my car when taking her to and from her apartment near the campus. It sounds a little ridiculous, but the church had really done a job on me and had made me extremely scrupulous. The seminary training had been to avoid women and even the occasion of sin or causing scandal, and I'd bought into that, hook, line, and sinker!

As I began to question my behavior, I began to recognize that it was natural for me to find some women attractive. I think my first real awareness of that came in 1963 when, as a priest, I attended my first high school class reunion. I had been ordained for seven years and had been gone from home for ten years prior to that (in the seminary). I enjoyed seeing classmates that I hadn't seen in seventeen years and was flattered by their attention and respect for my calling, even though most of them weren't Catholic.

Then, I was surprised to see the girl I had dated just before leaving for the seminary. I asked someone about her because I'd heard that she was married, but was at the reunion with another man. I was told that she had married someone from our high school and moved to California but she had divorced and was living with her two teenage boys in southern California. I spoke to her briefly at the reunion, but as the gathering was breaking up and everyone was leaving, I caught up with her at the doorway and we chatted briefly before she left with her escort.

A year later, I received a letter from her, saying that she was coming home to Saugus that summer and would be passing through Wisconsin. She asked if I'd mind if she and her boys stopped to see me, and I answered that I'd be delighted. My mother was keeping house for us at the Newman Center, so I told her of planned visit. In hindsight, I believe that my mother didn't approve of her coming. She felt that it might be dangerous. However, she never objected and helped me prepare a meal for them when they arrived. They stayed just one night at a nearby motel and left in the morning. I still had a deep fondness for her and couldn't help thinking about how things might have been if I hadn't been a priest.

Over the next couple years, I visited her twice while visiting California and on my second visit, I told her at dinner how I felt about her, but just as I'd done on our last date in high school, I again explained that I could never leave the priesthood. I believe she understood and respected my dedication.

We parted as friends, but as I was flying home the next day, I was terribly torn between my commitment to the priesthood and going back to her. Ironically, many years later (probably twenty-five years), I met her again by chance at a conference in Maine. I almost didn't recognize her, but I asked if she knew me—and she did. She had remarried and had another grown son. We exchanged pictures of our families and wished each other well. Then, shortly before our fiftieth high school reunion, I learned that she had died of cancer.

I'm including these very personal recollections in this book because I believe they reveal the struggle I went through in trying to live the life the church expected of me while, at the same time, responding to very real needs that had been repressed for such a long time. I felt guilty that I was human and wanted to share my life with another human being—a woman I could love and have a family with. I'd been told in the seminary that marriage was forbidden to us because we couldn't serve God adequately and the people He had entrusted to us if we were married and shared our lives with a wife.

Yes, there are men—and women—who have the vocation to celibate lives, but it's a special calling and not every priest has it. If celibacy is a gift, it can't be forced upon anyone, regardless of their state of life. For many years I've believed resolutely that there's no essential connection between celibacy and the priesthood. It's a manmade requirement, imposed by an all-male hierarchical institution for its own convenience and not because it was ever decreed by God.

Prior to meeting Jackie, my future wife, I met one or two other women I had feelings for and contemplated relationships with, but it wasn't until I met Jackie and came to know her well that I even considered leaving the clerical state to marry. At first, our relationship was awkward. We'd travel some distance from where we worked to have dinner, always fearful that we'd run into someone we knew and set tongues wagging.

I recall one such incident.

We were just entering a restaurant when Jackie suddenly gasped and said, "Oh, my! Let's get out of here right now."

She had seen a number of high school students from the parish where she'd taught school in Chippewa Falls. Fortunately, we left so quickly that they never saw us.

After one of those dinner dates, I decided that I'd send Jackie a bouquet of red roses. Jackie was taken back by that, but very pleased. She told a close lay friend who knew she was leaving and knew about the dinner dates.

Her friend's immediate comment was, "Jackie, do you really think his intentions are honorable?"

Jackie was a little hurt, but what could she say, except, "I certainly hope so."

A few years later, after our marriage, Jackie was visiting her mother and took a side trip to Chippewa Falls, where she had last taught school. She dropped in to see the friend who had made the remark about my intentions. By that time, all three of our children had been born and Jackie was carrying Jeff, our youngest, in her arms.

She couldn't resist saying, with just a trace of sarcasm, "Oh, by the way, Dorothy, I really do think Jim had honorable intentions!"

What a terrible way to carry on a courtship. By then, we knew our feelings for each other were real and that we must soon make a decision. Either I'd have to leave the clerical state and we'd marry or we'd have to break off our relationship, perhaps permanently!

Jackie was working in the diet office at a hospital in Marshfield, Wisconsin. My father was very ill in Alexandria, Virginia. We'd talked with my mother and we'd visited with Jackie's mother and father in Mountain, Wisconsin, about our plans. It only seemed right that we take a trip to my father's home, let him meet Jackie, and tell him of our plans to marry.

In the summer of 1970, Jackie attended her fourth year of summer school in religious education in Detroit, Michigan. I traveled out to see her one weekend and we firmed up our plans to travel east to see my father. We spent several days with him and my stepmother, Marion, at their summer home on Lake Louisa, near Charlottesville, Virginia. Before we got to Virginia, we made a detour through New England so Jackie could meet some of my friends on the East Coast and get a bird's eye view of New England.

Jim, Irene (Jackie's mother) and Jackie, 1970

When we returned to Wisconsin, we visited a few days with Jackie's parents and then went on to Marshfield and Stevens Point. During our trip home, we discussed our future and decided that we shouldn't see each other for a while so we could give serious thought to my leaving the clerical state. I was still struggling with that change in my life and what it would mean for both of us. We knew of other priests who had left and married, and we were aware of the trauma to themselves and their families. Were we ready to deal with the criticism of our families and friends and with being ostracized from the institutional church?

I was confused at that time about my feelings for Jackie. I believed that I cared for her deeply and wanted to be with her all of the time, but my training for the priesthood had made me feel extremely guilty about leaving the ministry that I'd worked so hard to achieve. I also didn't want to hurt my mother, whose life revolved about my being a priest. Could she ever understand my decision? I thought of her sacrifices after my father left and her refusal to even consider another permanent relationship. I knew that family members and friends would be disappointed and scandalized if I made such a decision. I agonized over the choices I had. Perhaps if I just waited a few months (or years), the church, motivated by major changes coming out of Vatican II, would reverse the requirement for compulsory lifetime celibacy.

It was less than two weeks before I called Jackie and asked her to meet me. We both knew that waiting any longer was just putting off the inevitable. We loved each other very much and walking away from that commitment just wasn't the right thing to do. We made the decision to marry in January 1971. I'd offer my last Masses for the students on the weekend of January 10th and we'd leave immediately afterward. Then we'd be married at Jackie's home on January 23rd.

Our plan was to drive to Washington, D.C., to see if I could get work with the federal government. I had decided not to see the bishop before I left, and after talking with one of the diocesan priests who'd left earlier and had gone in to see the bishop, I knew my decision was the right one.

The bishop, on hearing that the other priest was planning to marry, tried to dissuade him by saying, "Why don't you just take a leave of absence, go and get it out of your system, and then come back?"

That was the kind of morality we were dealing with from some bishops—and that was thirty-five years ago!

On January 11th, I gave my departure sermon, with Jackie in the congregation. Afterward, most of the students and faculty approved of my decision and some even wanted to go to the Bishop's home and ask him to let us stay on as their Newman chaplain. I explained that it would only serve as an embarrassment to everyone, and in the end, I'd have to leave anyway.

The following is the sermon I gave—with much sadness and a sense of loss—on January 11, 1971:

I Corinthians 13: "If I speak with the eloquence of man and of angels, but have no love, I become no more than blaring brass or crashing cymbal. If I have the gift of foretelling the future and hold in my mind not only all human knowledge but the very secrets of God, and if I have also that absolute faith, which can move mountains, but have no love, I amount to nothing at all. If I dispose of all that I possess, yes, even if I give my own body to be burned but have no love, I achieve precisely nothing.

"The love of which I speak is slow to lose patience—it looks for a way of being constructive. It is not possessive; it is neither anxious to impress nor does it cherish inflated ideas of its own importance.

"Love has good manners and does not pursue selfish advantage. It is not touchy. It does not keep account of evil or gloat over the wickedness of other people. On the contrary, it is glad with all good men when truth prevails.

"Love knows no limits to its endurance, no end to its trust, no fading of its hope; it can outlast anything. It is, in fact, the one thing that still stands when all else has fallen."

～

I think it was one of the Kennedy's, perhaps John, who once said, "A man, if he is to be a man, if he is to be a man at all, must risk doing what he believes has to be done."

Tonight, I have a task to perform which I would like to have avoided. This will be the most difficult, and probably the most important sermon of my life as a priest. It will be the last in the active ministry—at least for some time to come. I hope that you'll bear with me and weigh carefully what I have to say. It has taken months, very painful months, I can assure you, to arrive at this decision.

Twelve years ago, when most of you were just starting out on your educational careers, a long era in the history of the Catholic Church began to die, but hardly anyone would have guessed it at the time. All we knew was that Pius XII, a majestic, austere, and very intelligent pope, spiritual head for almost twenty years of over 500 million Roman Catholics, had died. At that time, in 1958, the church was truly "Mother Church," and we were docile children to be cared for, to be protected from the influences of the world—too controlled in our thinking (for our own good, of course), legal-minded in everything from observing the Eucharist fast to making special novenas of a set number of days and formulated prayers, to the absolute sinfulness of allowing any sexual feelings outside of marriage. We really believed that this *was* religion. This was what it meant to be a good Catholic, and we were contemptuous of Protestants and others who questioned our maturity and our virtue. I had been a priest only two years at that time, and I was typical. I was the epitome of conservatism, and I thought I always would be.

Like many others in 1958, I was disturbed, suspicious, and very critical of a man named Roncalli, a peasant priest—the complete opposite of Pius—a non-Roman in his thinking and experience who somehow received enough votes to become the new pope. He had none of the regal, painfully self-disciplined, emotionless stature of a Pius. Pope John was a misfit in the office of Peter. He was rather ugly and enormously fat, and he smiled most of the time. Good, well-groomed Catholics thought him to be quite senile. Why in God's name was the eighty-year-old cardinal, so unlike his predecessor, elected to such a noble office? Then someone suggested that he was just an interim pope—that is, someone harmless with little time left who could do little damage, until the church could discover someone of the stature of a Pius XII.

As we know, John lived less than five years as pope. He did only one really significant thing—opposed by most of his Roman advisors—he called for a world synod of bishops to discuss the problems of the entire world. Many obstacles were placed in the path of such a venture, but John persisted and the three-year council, with four sessions, turned the church inside out. John opened a Pandora's box that no one could ever hope to close without major changes in the structure and practice of the Catholic Church.

Under John's leadership, the church took on a new, very human, and loveable form. It stopped being so introspective and intramural in its thinking and began to look outside of itself to a world much bigger than itself, which was in desperate need of human, as well as divine, help.

John wrote two encyclical letters to the whole church that talked about real problems and their *real*, not theoretical, solutions. You might say that he resurrected the social gospel for Catholics, long used to the safety of a memorized catechism with all the "answers." John opened a window and he became the fresh air that was to energize the church into a complete reassessment of her, and he did this by simply letting people (everyone from prince to pauper) see that they were truly human, the clay of the earth, and servants of the People of God.

It will take historians a long time to evaluate John's pontificate and what followed him—and just what Vatican II really accomplished. Meanwhile, we continue to live in this historical period called the latter half of the twentieth century, and we all know that conflict rages within and outside of the church. The changes in the last decade have been traumatic, to say the least, and we've all been affected by them—like it or not.

Friends of long standing have quizzed me in recent years about my own change of attitude and conviction.

They say, "You've changed so much since we first knew you—how come?"

All I can answer is that I hope I've really changed, because that means growth. If I ever stop changing, then I'll be dead, and I don't want to die just yet. There's too much to be done—too much life to be lived yet—and somehow, I believe that I'm just beginning to really live for the first time—as a man and as a fully human being.

And this is what my talk today is all about, my friends. I am a human being. I can't be otherwise. I've honestly loved the priesthood and the kind of service that I've been privileged to give for the last fifteen years, and interestingly enough, to your age group for thirteen of those fifteen years. I've loved you as my friends. I don't really want to leave you. I have good memories of Eau Claire for eleven years, and two here at Stevens Point. You've all helped me more than you'll probably ever know. Your youthful spirit, sense of daring, openness to new ideas, your imagination, and your response to love have kept me young—at least in mind and heart.

But tonight, I'm speaking to you for the last time. This is the greatest challenge of my life, and although I know that some would rather I had left quietly and without a word to anyone, I need to have this time with you and I sincerely believe with all my heart that you need to hear what I'm saying to you. I ask only one favor from you. Believe in my integrity as a person and a priest. Believe that I'm doing what I believe has to be done. I don't expect all of you to accept my decision, but please give me the same benefit of doubt that I'd give you, and I believe that I've been that fair to you. This is a personal decision that I had to make so I could continue to be what I've asked you always to be—honest.

If we've done anything of worth here in these past two years, thanks in great part to Fr. Joe Sullivan, as well as Sr. Margaret Elsen, Fr. Vaughn Brockman, and all the others who've been so helpful, then I charge you tonight to see that it continues. You have nothing to be apologetic about. We have a great Newman community here, and it's up to you to see to it that it continues and gets better.

I'm leaving the active ministry only because the present law of the church forbids a married clergy. There's nothing essential between priesthood and celibacy. This is a disciplinary law that came into being late in the church's history and has been a point of controversy in every century.

I do love the faith—that faith which you and I share. I believe in the church, and in you as God's people. I'm not leaving the priesthood as I understand the sacrament I received almost fifteen years ago. No one can take that away from me. It's as permanent as a true marriage.

I do intend to marry soon. This hasn't been a hasty decision. I've known Jacquelyn Kresse for more than a year. She's been a source of great strength and encouragement to me as I struggled with this decision.

Several months before we met, she made a similar decision—equally difficult. She left the Notre Dame Order after serving with that community for thirteen years. I'm not ashamed to tell you that I love her very much. I'm sad to think that it took so long for me to let someone love me. She's given me more personal happiness than I ever thought possible. I can no longer accept the church's insistence on a celibate clergy—if this means denying my love for her. I can see no serious reason why I shouldn't be allowed to continue in my present capacity. I can't believe that my effectiveness as a minister of the church could be diminished by such an addition to my life—and so you see my dilemma.

In brief, I'll no longer be allowed to serve you in this community or to function as a priest in public gatherings. Officially, Jackie and I will be cut off from the institutional church—but we can never be cut off from you, the people.

I could have asked for a dispensation from my vows, which in essence would have been a request to be returned to the lay state. This I couldn't do, because I simply don't believe in such a process, and I doubt very sincerely that there are many who *do* believe in such a process.

In talking to many men about this, they've admitted that the dispensation was requested for the sake of the parents and friends so as not to hurt the people around them. I'm in no position to criticize their decision. However, it's contrary to my own and therefore I'd be a hypocrite if I requested something that is abhorrent to me.

I wanted to be a priest, and I want to remain a priest forever. I never wanted celibacy. It was a requirement I had to accept in order to be ordained. Knowing what I know now, I would never have been able to accept the priesthood under those conditions—conditions which are dehumanizing, to say the least.

My plans are to move to Washington, D.C., where Jackie and I will live while I'm interviewing for a job with the government. I'm fortunate that the kindness of close friends has made it possible for us to be without financial problems for at least four months while I carry out my job campaign. I know that it will be difficult to find work that can even approach in satisfaction what the priesthood has meant to me. But I see this as a great opportunity to grow in my Christian vocation and to come to understand people and their problems better than I've ever done as one who has been taken care of by a worshipping community.

I'm grateful for what I've received and my only hope is that both Jackie and I can continue to serve human beings. Together we've given almost thirty years of service to the church. I hope that will be remembered as people discuss the fact of our departure.

This is all I have to say. I'll close with the hope and with the challenge to you—that you as laymen won't sit back now and bemoan the choice we and others have made, but that you'll begin to make your own voices heard in urging those in authority to be courageous leaders and to use all the power and authority they have to change what has to be to changed in order for the church of this century to adequately serve the needs of all.

If this parish has been influenced by our words and actions among you, you'll become a voice of the future and you'll make those changes that only men can make.

～

I ended my sermon with a quote from Vatican II on the laity: "Upon all the laity, therefore, rests the noble duty of working to extend the divine plan of salvation ever increasingly to all men of each epoch and in every land.

"Consequently, let every opportunity be given them so that, according to their abilities and the needs of the times, they may zealously participate in the saving work of the church. An individual layman, by reason of the knowledge, competence, or outstanding ability which he may enjoy, is permitted and sometimes even obliged to express his opinion on things which concern the good of the church."

～

I sent a telegram to the bishop on Sunday evening, telling him of my decision. I wouldn't let him interfere with my last remarks to the group of people I had served and loved. Then I turned over the responsibility to the assistant Newman chaplain, who was Fr. Joe Sullivan's replacement.

Sister Margaret Elsen, who was one of the few people who knew beforehand that I was leaving, remained. God bless her, she stood by us and even took up an informal collection to help us with the difficulties we were sure to encounter during the coming months. Jackie and I have remained close to her all through our marriage and thirty-five years later, she's still one of our best friends.

After Mass, Jackie was standing in the entry. A young mother approached her with her two small children.

The woman told her children, "This is the lady Father Jim is going to marry."

Then she gave Jackie a card with $25 in it. It was only many years later that Jackie told me of that kind gesture.

CHAPTER SEVEN

TODAY IS THE FIRST DAY OF THE REST OF OUR LIVES

We obtained our marriage license, and on January 23, 1971, we pronounced our vows to each other with Fr. Joe and the Lutheran pastor on campus officiating. As planned, we were married in Jackie's home. My mother was too sick to attend and my father, also recuperating from an illness, was too far away. Jackie's mother helped with the arrangements and her father, who'd had a serious stroke some time back, looked on. My brother and his wife, Jackie's two brothers, and one sister-in-law, along with a few close friends were our congregation.

Our wedding, Mountain, Wisconsin, January 23, 1971

The following are excerpts from our marriage, taken from the program we have as a momento of the occasion. I believe it's important to hear the vows we shared and the messages we wanted conveyed at our own marriage. It will offer a better understanding of the passion and conviction that we both put into our present ministry to others.

Opening Song ("Today," sung by Jackie)
Final verse
Today while the blossoms still cling to the vine,
I'll taste your strawberries, I'll drink your sweet wine.
A million tomorrows shall all pass away ere I forget all the joy that is mine, today.

Prayer of St. Francis
Lord, make me an instrument of Your Peace
Where there is hatred, let me show Love
Where there is injury, pardon
Where there is doubt, faith
Where there is despair, hope
Where there is darkness, light
Where there is sadness, joy

Scripture Readings
Ecclesiasticus 26: 1–4
Happy the husband of a really good wife. The number of his days will be doubled.

A perfect wife is the joy of her husband. He will live out the years of his life in peace. A good wife is the best of portions, reserved for those who fear the Lord. Rich or poor, they will be glad of heart, cheerful of face, whatever the season.

St. John's Prologue
At the beginning God expressed himself...

Contemporary Reading (from *The Prophet*)
And a youth said, "Speak to us of friendship."
And he answered, saying: Your friend is your needs answered.
…

The Gloria (All together)
Marriage Ceremony

Invitation to Pronounce Marriage Vows
Song ("Into Your Hands")
Into your hands we commend our spirit, O Lord,
Into Your hands we commend our hearts,

…

Vows (Jim)
Jacquelyn Corrine Kresse, I love you and am proud to say this in the presence of witnesses. May God, our Father, our parents, and all those who have come here today to share our great joy be witnesses to the vows we freely make to each other.

Jackie, I, James Edward Lovejoy, publicly take you as my wife and joyfully promise to intensify that love which we have already pledged to each other.

I sincerely believe that those vows, once spoken in the religious life, have not been renounced or revoked by this new vocation of marriage, but are further sanctified, renewed, and fulfilled in our present union.

Vows (Jackie)
I, Jacquelyn Corrine Kresse, am happy to accept the love that you, James Edward Lovejoy, have promised me. In the presence of my family and others who love us, I promise to be your wife—to be friend to you, to love you, and to help you fulfill your dreams.

I ask that the love that has grown between us may increase each day and strengthen us to be the persons Our Father has planned us to be.

Solemn Declaration of Matrimonial Consent (Celebrant, Jim Schneider)

Blessing of Rings (Jim)

May God bless this symbol of our marriage promises; may this ring be a constant reminder to us that, like gold, our union is a precious thing and must be respected. May the unbroken circle remind us that this decision is forever and has no end—just new beginnings.

Finally, may its prominent position on the third finger of the left hand tell the whole world of our love and be a reassurance to all we meet that we will always be ready and willing to help others.

Blessing of Rings (Jackie)

Wear this ring, Jim, as a sign of my love. May it ever remind you, as it serves to remind others, that there is always someone who loves you. May this ring, like the four seasons of the year, remind us that love never ends, but is ever renewed and after every winter there is a spring and the birth of new hope.

Prayers of Intention (All participate, Joe Sullivan lead)
Prayer of Encouragement (Joe Sullivan and Jim Schneider)
Preparation of the Gifts (Bread and Wine) by Jim and Jackie
Take Our Bread
Take our bread, we as You, take our hearts, we love You;
Take our lives, O Father, we are Yours, we are Yours.
Yours as we stand at the table You set;
Yours as we eat the bread our Hearts can't forget.
We are the sign of Your life with us yet. We are Yours, we are Yours.

Your holy people standing washed in Your blood, Spirit-filled yet hungry

We await Your food.

We are poor, but we've brought ourselves the best we could.

We are Yours, we are Yours.

Canon of the Mass

Preface

Father, we praise You for all the good things You have done in our midst, for giving us life in this world and a promise of life with You forever.

We praise You and thank You for giving us other human beings to love and grow with. Especially, we thank You for the love You have implanted in the hearts of men and women that they may share a common life of service to You.

Jim and Jackie thank You for the gift of their love and devotion to each other. They now consecrate it in this wedding liturgy and join with the whole human race in praising Your goodness.

Canon

We are here in the home of Jacquelyn Kresse Lovejoy, where she and her family welcome James Edward Lovejoy and his family to the Christian celebration which has united Jim and Jackie in the loving bond of marriage.

We offer our common worship to God, our Father, in thanksgiving for this truly holy event. May the whole church, all God's people join with us in our joy.

May all of us use this occasion to renew our own relationships of love and service to each other and in a special way may our relationship to Christ, our Brother, be a source of strength and encouragement. It is His sacrifice of love for us that we celebrate once again. It was His role as servant that we wish to imitate.

May Jackie and Jim continue to serve Him as they unite themselves in this sacrament. Their past vows of Christian service are now intensified in this new vocation. Let this celebration be pleasing to One who is Love itself.

Consecration

It was in the form of a servant that our Lord shared His last meal with friends. He wished to remain with them in a new way. Because His physical presence would be denied them, He took common bread from the table where they were eating, blessed it, broke it into pieces, and gave it to His friends, saying: "Take and eat. This is my body. It is being given up in sacrifice for you."

And after each one had eaten, He took a cup of wine from the table, blessed this, and passed it around the table for each one to drink, saying, "Take and drink, for this is the cup of my blood. It is blood of the new and everlasting contract with my people, which for you and for all men will be shed until all sins are forgiven. Whenever you repeat this celebration, do it always in my memory."

We have now completed our renewal of His sacrificial love. In thanksgiving for His living among us, we wish to share His Eucharistic Presense by communicating from each other's hands—His Body and Blood. In this way, we demonstrate faith in our union with Him and with each other.

May what we have done benefit all men, those present at this celebration, especially the newly united couple and their families and all men everywhere who acknowledge His love for us and their own needs.

We pray for all those who love us and could not be here because of distance, illness, or death. May they be here in spirit and reap with us the rich fruits of this glorious day.

Holy Father, be pleased with what we have done in Your name. We ask this in union with Your Son and the Holy Spirit—One God forever—amen.

The Lord's Prayer (All together)

The Sign of Peace is Given to all by Jackie and Jim

Communion (Administered under both species to all who wish to communicate)

Final Prayer and Blessing, (Celebrant, Joe Sullivan)

Closing Song ("Today is the First Day of the Rest of Our Lives")
And I remind you your befores are all behind you,
And we're living in the now.
And we'll deal with tomorrow, when tomorrow arrives.
Till then, today is the first day of the rest of our lives.

~

On top of the World

We had a brief honeymoon in Rhinelander, Wisconsin. I think it snowed every day, and at night we had to stuff towels in the windows and under the doors of our cabin to keep out the drifts, but we were happy just to be together and looked forward with great enthusiasm to the adventure we would share in the coming months and years. The decision to marry had been a difficult one, but we've never regretted it.

We packed all of our belongings in my car and filled a small U-Haul. We stopped to visit with my mother and then headed to Milwaukee for a party that some friends had planned for us. Somehow we managed to get through some freezing weather and a blizzard and headed East. When we reached Washington, D.C., we went out to Ft. Belvoir to see my father, who was convalescing from a serious operation. Then we drove to a former Maryknoll classmate's home. He had recently returned from Guatemala and had also left the clerical state. We stayed with him for a few days while we did some apartment hunting.

All of our belongings in a 4x6 UHaul on our way to Washington, DC

A friend of ours from Stevens Point had given us a generous gift and with that money, along with the money Sr. Margaret had raised on our behalf, we felt we could get by for awhile, at least until I landed a job. Little did we know then that it would take four months for me to be hired by the Defense Department.

Our first apartment was in Maryland. We really wanted to live in Virginia, but Maryland would have to do until we found an apartment closer to Washington. Shortly after we got settled, my brother George came to in Washington on business and stayed overnight with us. We were pleased to have him as our first guest.

Within a few weeks, we found an apartment in Alexandria, Virginia, and moved for the second time. That apartment was larger and closer to the city where I hoped to find work. Thus began an odyssey that tested our faith and commitment to the new life we'd chosen.

Our first apartment in Virginia, 1971

Jackie was terrific. She insisted that I look upon my job search as my first job, so each day I'd leave the house in the morning and travel by bus into the district where I'd managed to get a couple interviews. I never left an interview without asking for at least one referral. At home each evening, I'd put the interviews I'd had that day on a large chart. Then I'd type up my memories of the interview and the referrals I'd received. It was a tedious effort, but we were determined to find work at a level that would support us.

I always told prospective employers about my background and found that almost everyone was sympathetic and supportive, even if they had no immediate job opportunities for me. Over the next four months, there were some real disappointments, and it was difficult for us not to get discouraged.

One job prospect came from an unusual contact and would ultimately result in my first job with the government, but only after frustrating months of waiting day to day for the call that would put me to work.

Shortly before leaving Stevens Point, I had officiated at a wedding of two college students. They had received one of many letters I sent out to relatives, friends, and acquaintances, asking for job referrals. One day, I received a letter from that couple, saying that they were concerned about my difficulty in finding work. The husband's father had worked in local politics with Melvin Laird, the current Secretary of Defense at the Pentagon in Washington, D.C. They had talked to his dad about my plight and had asked him if there was anything he might be able to do to help. He agreed to do what he could, and the couple wanted me to know that I might be hearing from him (or one of his aides) in the next few weeks.

We watched the mail over the next couple weeks until one night we received a call from Robert Froehlke, also from Stevens Point and formerly president of Sentry Insurance, a large insurance firm in that city. He was one of Mr. Laird's top administrators and he told us that Mr. Laird had asked him to get in touch with us. He asked about my background and interests and said he'd arrange a meeting with his administrative assistant, Russell Knauss. He couldn't guarantee a job right away, but assured me that Mr. Knauss would do all he could to be of help.

Jackie and I were ecstatic! After a full month of interviews and coming up against a stone wall, that was the first positive news we'd had. Without knowing where it would lead, we were optimistic, so it was about then (George Washington's birthday) that we went out and splurged on a new black-and-white 12-inch TV set. Certainly I would be working for the government within the next few weeks.

It was early in March when I came home one day from a number of interview sessions in Washington to find Jackie with a broad smile on her face. She'd been to see the doctor about what she thought might be the flu—but it wasn't the flu. She was pregnant with our first child!

We could hardly contain ourselves with joy. We hadn't thought it would happen so soon, but we were ready for a family—something we'd wanted from day one. The only problem was that I was still unemployed. We needed to step up my job search and have at least one back-up to my possible employment with the Department of Defense. At that time, I was in a holding pattern there. I knew they intended to hire me, but could do nothing until the Congressional Appropriations Committee had approved a budget for that program. I called the temporary office they'd set up in Rosslyn just about every week.

If I was able to talk to Colonel Krise, the director, I'd get very positive news, indicating that the program was about to be approved and that it was only a matter of time. If I talked to his deputy, an Air Force colonel, I heard a more pessimistic viewpoint. The deputy, also a colonel, was black and understandably much more skeptical about the Defense Department's seriousness in dealing with race relations in the military. He doubted that they'd ever concede to spend the money on such a social action program.

That was a critical period in our marriage. We were about to have a family, yet our money was running out and I had no idea when I'd receive my first paycheck. It was only our faith in God and in each other that kept us forging ahead.

Jackie did a great job with budgeting our meager funds and preparing meals that were adequate but inexpensive. We never went out to eat, and our only entertainment was a movie once a month at a theater in Crystal City, Virginia, that offered movies for a dollar.

Speaking of race relations, I'll never forget the night we attended a movie in the District, starring Sydney Poitier, titled *Brother John*. It was the story of a young black man who had come back to the southern town where he was raised to attend his grandmother's funeral. It was a violent movie depicting how cruel whites were to black people in the days prior to the Civil Rights movement.

As the film went on and Sydney underwent beatings and was almost lynched, the crowd in the theater roared their support for the hero as he fought off his attackers .It was then that I realized that Jackie and I were the only white faces in a sea of black. I began to perspire and wondered if we'd get out of the theater alive. Finally, the movie ended with Poitier being vindicated and conquering his white oppressors.

I said to Jackie, "Let's get out of here as quickly as possible."

Jackie looked at me and calmly said, "OK, but I need to use the bathroom on the way out."

"Oh, my God," I thought.

Couldn't she just hold it until we were out of the District? But I learned something that night that would stay with me for the next 35 years—Jackie always needs to use the bathroom before we leave any event! I stood at the back of the theater and tried to appear as inconspicuous as possible while the theater emptied out. I expected to be beaten to a pulp at any moment as a representative of the white crackers who had made Sydney's life so miserable in the movie.

We made it to our car in one piece and drove home safely—no thanks to my wife, who just smiled and said, "Wasn't that a wonderful movie? I'm so happy we saw it!"

It was sometime in April that we got another little boost in my job search. After one of my interviews, I received a phone call telling me that I was being considered for a job with the Bureau of Indian Affairs. There was a new program starting up in Albuquerque, New Mexico, and they had three GS-13 positions available. It was the same grade level of the job with the Defense Department, so I was very interested. They asked me to come in for another interview and as a result, I was offered one of the positions.

The only drawback was that it would be a temporary appointment for a year. If the program was successful, I would likely be hired fulltime. Jackie and I talked it over and weighed the advantages of both jobs. The offer was only a temporary hire, but at least it was a job, and one that would pay quite well—at least for the next year. Then there would be a good chance that it would become permanent. They told me that I'd have to make up my mind in three days (over the weekend) since they had to fill the positions immediately.

I leaned toward the Defense Department position. The following Monday morning, I called Colonel Krise and told him of my other offer. He didn't try to tell me what I should do, but he assured me that the appropriations bill was close to being signed. He added that he hoped I'd choose to wait, but he understood my dilemma and our need for immediate income.

After hours of deliberation and prayer, we decided to bite the bullet and hold out for the Defense Department job and fortunately, we made the right choice. Within a month and a half, I was hired by the Defense Race Relations Institute as an education advisor and instructor. The BIA job only lasted for a year—and then the program was terminated.

Then came some very sad news. Jackie's mother called to say that Jackie's dad had had another, more severe, stroke. The doctors didn't offer much hope that he'd recover and advised Mrs. Kresse to gather his family as quickly as possible. Naturally, we dropped everything and set out by car for Wisconsin. Jackie kept tabs on her father's condition along the way and unfortunately, he passed away while we were en route. Her mother told us that he had been unconscious most of the time and probably wouldn't have recognized anyone in his condition.

My mother was also sick at the time, but resting comfortably at Sacred Heart Hospital in Eau Claire, so I left Jackie at her home and drove to Eau Claire to see my mom. Once assured that she was doing well and expected to go home soon, I returned to be with Jackie and her family for her dad's funeral.

I arrived just in time to enter the church with them. Jackie and her mother were happy to see me. Jackie feels now that it was my effort to be at her dad's funeral that caused a huge change in her dad's sister, Aunt Jo's, attitude toward us and ultimately resulted in her open acceptance of our marriage. Up to that point, she had wanted to have nothing to do with either of us because of my leaving the clerical state and marrying Jackie, contrary to the will of the church.

Shortly thereafter, we returned to Virginia and I resumed my job search, ever mindful that I had to have some kind of work soon or we'd be flat broke. At that time, another incident took place that almost caused a serious break with my father.

We were getting desperate as we came to the end of May, the fourth month since our arrival in Washington. I really didn't want to ask my father for any financial support, but with the baby coming and no income coming in, I felt that I had to do something drastic. So one night I went to see my father at his home in Alexandria and told him that I'd been assured that a job with DOD was imminent, but needed some help in the interim.

To my surprise, he refused and began to lecture me on my failure to be responsible, even chastising me (and George) for not taking more responsibility for my mother's welfare while leaving it up to him to care for her all those years. I couldn't understand his logic, since he'd been the one who left our mother to marry another woman. Since there had never been a formal divorce, how could he feel that it wasn't his responsibility to continue to care for her and to provide living expenses? How had that suddenly become either George's or my responsibility? I left a short time later and returned home, angry and perplexed.

If it hadn't been for Jackie's intervention, I probably would never have seen my father again, but she wasn't entirely unsympathetic. Jackie felt that it had been my dad's way of getting some issues on the table and that he probably felt as badly as I did that it had created tension between us. She suggested that we invite my dad and Marion to join us for supper the following week and treat the incident as though it had never occurred. I guess that my pride was hurt, but I agreed that she was probably right and left it up to her to offer the invitation. To my surprise, they accepted, and we had dinner together the following week—and our dispute was never mentioned.

I decided the next day to go down to the Montgomery Ward store and see if I could gain some temporary employment. At least we'd have some income coming in. Our bank account was just about empty and we had another month's rent due in a few days.

Then suddenly everything changed. I received an unexpected call from Colonel Krise. The appropriations bill had been signed and the Defense Race Relations Institute was in business. They'd bring me on as the first civilian employee—but only as a temporary hire. However, once I was on board, it would be relatively easy to make my appointment permanent.

He asked me to come in the next day and sign the necessary papers. After four months of agonizing, and trying to live on love alone, we could finally begin to breathe freely and make some plans for the future.

During that bleak period, I'd been attending weekly seminars with other resigned priests at a location in Washington under the direction of a former Jesuit priest. He was tough on us and insisted that we take our search and our credentials seriously. He said that after leaving the clerical system, too many priests were satisfied to take just about any job, feeling that the priesthood had prepared them for no other career.

He impressed on us that our education (8–10 years of seminary training) and our experience as priests in education, pastoral counseling, preaching, organizing events, and administering parish finances, put us in the same category as other young professionals. We were equally qualified to find employment at a mid-executive level or at a GS-13–15 government level.

"Don't underestimate yourselves!" he insisted.

There were times when we wanted to say, "He's nuts! We'll never get a job if we listen to him."

However, John would bring resigned priests, married and single, to our meetings who'd already done just what John said we could do, and they gave us pep talks to keep us pressing ahead.

I have no idea how many men like myself John Mulholland helped during the late 60s and early 70s, when several thousand priests left the active ministry with no help from the institution. I believe that the hierarchy just hoped that we'd all go away and be forgotten. (How ironic that it was during those same years that many of the country's bishops were, unbeknownst to most of us, moving pedophile priests from parish to parish, hiding their crimes from the public and at the same time paying for their recuperation, their salaries, and their retirement benefits.)

When I received my first check from the federal government in mid-June 1971, we felt that we deserved to celebrate with our first expensive meal in months. We made reservations at the George Washington Inn, a swank restaurant in Alexandria, Virginia, and I don't believe either of us ever enjoyed a steak so much! We weren't on Easy Street, but our long journey to find work was over at last, and we'd worry about tomorrow— tomorrow!

I was fortunate to have landed a GS-13 position during a Republican administration (Nixon's). It was also fortunate that no one gave a damn about my political allegiance. I started working immediately, along with the officers who were already on board, to develop a curriculum for the new institute.

There would be two major divisions: Behavioral Science, which would include such subjects as Institutional Racism, Attitudes and Behavior, and Games People Play; and Ethnic Studies, including Afro-Americans, Native Americans, and Appalachia. There would be lectures on each of those subjects, small group discussions involving a variety of ethnic backgrounds, and a series of inner city experiences to give military instructors and their pupils a firsthand look at racial diversity in America.

The first order of business for Colonel Krise and his staff was to locate a place for the Institute to be housed. There were several options, including Benjamin Harrison Army Base in Indiana. However, Colonel Krise finally settled on Patrick Air Force Base in Cocoa Beach, Florida. We all guessed that the decision was due in part to the colonel's love of sailing. Ultimately, he sailed his forty-foot sailboat down the intercoastal seaway and parked it in a docking space on Merritt Island.

The colonel was an interesting person—rather hard to get to know, but very fair. It was one of his last commands before his retirement. He'd been a tank commander in Europe during World War II, and the last we heard of him, he and his wife were operating a day-sailing business, based out of St. Thomas in the Caribbean.

Once we had the location settled and it had been approved by the Pentagon, several of us were sent to make preliminary preparations so the institute could set up shop. Shortly before my departure, Mr. Froehlke, who was now Secretary of the Army, invited Jackie and me to pay him a visit on E-Ring at the Pentagon.

We were thrilled, and once we'd found his office and had gone through the usual protocol, we enjoyed nearly a half hour with him. He was most cordial, providing coffee and refreshments and showing great interest in the fact that we were awaiting parenthood before the end of the year. He also talked about his own family and assured us that we'd have our happiest moments with our children, even though they'd undoubtedly give us some hair-raising moments as they grew to adulthood.

One of his secretaries interrupted our visit and soon afterward Mr. Froehlke had to bring our meeting to a close. Jackie always recalls his words, in which he apologized for leaving us due to a scheduled meeting with the joint chiefs in five minutes.

He whispered to Jackie, "I'd much rather continue our visit, but duty calls!"

Late in August, I drove alone to Cocoa Beach. I'd return for Jackie on Labor Day weekend. Once I'd located Patrick AFB and the building we were to occupy, I started looking for a place to live, at least temporarily. I was fortunate to find a small cluster of Spanish-style cottages called Casa Del Sol along Route 1-A in Indiatlantic, about twelve miles from the base. The best part was that the cottages were right across the highway from the Atlantic Ocean.

I could hardly wait to show Jackie our first real home. The cottage was small, with a living room, two bedrooms, a kitchen, and a bath, but it was a real step up from the apartment where we'd been living in Arlington. We even had air conditioning units in each room, so we wouldn't have to rope an old AC unit to the window!

I returned to Washington just before Labor Day. My father had arranged for my mother to move to the area. He didn't want George or me to have to worry about her in Wisconsin. While George and I agreed with his plan at the time, it turned out to be a big mistake. My mother would have been much better off with the friends she'd made in Wisconsin, but how could we have known?

Jackie had flown out to get my mother and bring her back while I was in Florida. They stayed with my cousin and his wife in Virginia until my return. My mother was staying temporarily in a motel in Alexandria when Jackie and I started our trip to Florida over Labor Day weekend. She'd soon be moving to an apartment in Maryland that my father had found for her. We assumed that she couldn't live in Virginia, where my father and his second wife lived, because legally he could have been charged with bigamy. It wasn't a very happy time for any of us.

When Jackie and I drove through Cocoa Beach, Florida, she wasn't impressed and could only visualize our living in one of the old gray tenement houses that lined the highway. I tried to assure her that where we were headed was much better, but I could tell that she was nervous and not too optimistic. Once we crossed the bridge onto Rt. 1-A and headed south along the ocean, however, she breathed a sigh of relief, and when we drove into the Casa Del Sol subdivision and stopped in front of our cottage, she was delighted.

She immediately fell in love with the place, just as I had, and we anxiously moved our few belongings inside. It was to be the first of many homes we'd either rent or own over the next thirty-five years. But at that moment, it felt like a castle!

Our first class of about one hundred military students was to arrive in a few short weeks, and there was a great deal of work ahead of us to prepare for their arrival. All the staff was now on board and some additional civilian employees had been hired. I shared a large office with Army Colonel Ralph Morgan, the Director of Education. He was a jovial man, also in one of his last assignments prior to retirement, and we got along well. I enjoyed his company and appreciated his patience with my lack of experience.

Two research people were soon added to the staff. A senior education advisor, a black professor from the University of Pittsburgh, had been hired and would be joining us shortly. I'd be working for him.

CHAPTER EIGHT
WE ARE A FAMILY

Jackie and I enjoyed those first few weeks of our new home in Florida. We took advantage of the beach and anxiously looked forward to the arrival of our first child. Jackie had great confidence in her new physician, Dr. Madry. (Actually, I had selected him from among others in the phone book because his office was the only one that answered when I called on my lunch hour during my pre-visit to Florida.) He saw her the day after we arrived on Labor Day weekend and told her that the baby should arrive on November 1, 1971—the same day that our first DRRI Class was scheduled to begin at the institute.

The class started on time, but our baby wasn't ready to greet the world. She arrived some seventeen days late, on November 17th. Jackie's mother, Irene, had come from Wisconsin to be with her daughter and new grandchild.

I must add a note here about our puppy, Linus, which we named after a character in the "Peanuts" comic strip. I brought him home after Jackie's first false alarm trip to the hospital. When I told the DRRI staff the next day that we had an addition to the Lovejoy family, they all thought Jackie had delivered.

I said, "Oh, no! Not yet. I was referring to our new puppy!"

We remember vividly the night Jackie went into the hospital. I had gone to bed early because of some long days at the institute and a late counseling session for one of the DRRI staff members. Jackie was watching TV in the living room and Linus was at her feet. When

Jackie's water broke, the poor dog was drenched—but he lived through it!

We hurried Jackie to the hospital, and then came the hours of waiting—we waited through the night and were impatiently waiting on the morning of November 17th. I had just gone into the bathroom when Jackie's mother called to me, saying that the baby was on the way. In those days, fathers weren't allowed in the delivery room, so I wasn't a witness to Jennifer's birth, but I soon heard her welcome cries, and before long the doctor emerged to say that we had a healthy baby girl. Both mother and child were doing fine.

Our first child, Jennifer, born in Melbourne, Florida, November 17, 1971)

As I'm sure every parent will attest, the arrival of one's first child is probably the most remarkable and thrilling event in one's life. You suddenly realize that you and your wife have been the instruments through which God has created a new life, forever bound up with yours, but nevertheless a separate human being. Nothing in the universe can match that moment—not even Neil Armstrong's first step on the moon! I've often thought, since we were blessed with two more children, that while the priesthood was very special and always will be part of the chronology of my life, even that can't match the gift of life in which we've so intimately participated.

We were now a family. Up until that moment, we were two people very much in love and caring deeply for each other, but now we had a new responsibility, and our lives would never be the same. What a pity that the Catholic Church hierarchy can't understand that simple truth. It's not that celibacy is wrong. For a very few gifted people who receive the special grace to live without benefit of family and can dedicate themselves solely to God, celibacy is a true calling, but not necessarily a sacramental vocation—as is priesthood and matrimony.

Jim and Jennifer at home, Daddy's Little Girl

Why shouldn't those two vocations be available to the same individuals, whether they be man or woman? For those of us who've

89

been ordained priests and are now also married, there's no intrinsic obstacle to serving both with fidelity and commitment. If celibacy is truly a requirement for ordination, why were one or more of the apostles married, and why did the early church allow married priests, bishops—and even popes—from the earliest days of Christianity until the mid-twelfth century?

Even Pope John Paul II, while not allowing bishops of the worldwide church to even discuss the requirement of celibacy for ordination, stated in one of his early pronouncements, that there is no essential connection between the priesthood and celibacy.

Since we moved to Florida the same year that Disney World arrived in Orlando, we thought that we should be two of the first visitors to the theme park, so we visited in October 1971, just prior to the birth of our first child. As Jackie recalls, we thought the exercise of walking around may induce labor, but it took another month for the baby to arrive. We were later to visit the park on a number of occasions with our growing family. We fondly remember Jennifer's excitement when we went through one of the exhibits and listened to what would become her favorite tune, "It's a Small World After All."

When the first class at the institute graduated, our staff and faculty were flown from Patrick AFB to Key West, where senior members from the Pentagon met with us for several days to review the results of an analysis. They were sufficiently satisfied with what we'd accomplished and with some suggested changes; Colonel Krise was given the go-ahead to prepare for subsequent classes. The institute was in business, and we readied ourselves for several fourteen-week sessions in 1972.

About the same time, I received word from my father that things weren't going so well with my mother's move from Wisconsin. He was doing the best he could to help her with what she needed, but his own health was deteriorating and he didn't know how much longer he could continue traveling back and forth from Virginia to Maryland where she had her apartment. She was also becoming homesick for her friends in Wisconsin and feeling isolated and abandoned. He admitted that his plan to bring her east to care for her wasn't working out.

Jackie and I talked about it and decided that we should ask her to come to Florida to live with us. If she became stronger and more independent, perhaps she could take an apartment near us and maintain her independence. It was out of the question to ask George and Marilyn to have her come to Chicago. They had four very young boys and George was struggling with two jobs to make ends meet.

Consequently, I flew to Washington shortly before Thanksgiving, helped my mother dispose of some things she wouldn't need in Florida, and flew back with her. She seemed disoriented while we were preparing to return, but once on the plane she seemed to cheer up and actually looked forward to joining us. Our small cottage suddenly became crowded, and we knew that our plan to move into our own home couldn't be put off.

We immediately started looking for a home on the mainland. Melbourne seemed to be a nice community and closer to the base, so we concentrated on finding something suitable. We were fortunate to find a reasonably priced home not far from Route 1 in a new subdivision. An older couple was in the process of moving further south into a mobile home park. Jackie often recalled that it was the easiest of all the moves we were to make over the next thirty years. They offered to sell us just about all their furniture, and since we had little furniture of our own, that worked out well for us—and for them.

As Jackie put it, "All we had to do was buy a few groceries, make our bed, and move right in."

We now had a room for my mother and one for the baby, as well as a bedroom of our own, right next to the nursery. In retrospect, it's hard to believe that we only paid $19,500 for the home, carport, and fenced backyard with fruit trees and a sprinkler system. All the furniture, including a large color TV (quite a luxury after our apartment in Virginia) only cost us $2,000 more.

CHAPTER NINE
IN GOOD TIMES AND BAD

In early 1972, Jackie and I felt that we needed to get away for a couple days with Jennifer. My mother seemed reasonably well and assured us that she'd be fine. We asked the couple who lived next door to look in on her periodically and they said they'd be delighted to do so.

I had told Jackie how impressed I was with Key West, where I'd attended the meeting with the Pentagon brass, so we decided to make the same trip, so she could see what I was talking about. The trip was uneventful but, unfortunately, we had picked the coldest weekend on record, or so it seemed. We weren't dressed for the drop in temperature, so only Jennifer was comfortable in the clothing we'd brought along for her and her baby blankets. However, despite the unseasonable weather for that subtropical area, we managed to enjoy the trip and came home relaxed and ready to get back to work.

In mid-April, we decided that it was time for Jackie to make another trip, this time alone with our daughter. My mother had been in and out of the hospital, but seemed to be doing fairly well. On the other hand, reports on my father weren't good and we wanted him to see his only granddaughter. Late in the month, they flew to Washington, D.C., and my father managed to pick them up at the airport to bring them home for a visit. As Jackie said later, it was a beautiful visit. My father was delighted to have them, and Marion made them feel right at home.

In the meantime, I'd been told that my mother could come home from the hospital after a short stay. She enjoyed playing with Jennifer very much. My mother, having had us three boys and then having watched George's four boys grow up, longed for a little girl. The few months she spent with us were happy ones for her, if for no other reason than she had a little girl to spoil. Jackie tells of the great pleasure my mother took in buying Jennifer her first pair of (as she called them) fancy pants!

Jackie, Jennifer, and my mother, Marie

The next few weeks were a blur in my mind and difficult to talk about even now. I couldn't stay at home with my mother, so when she became sick again, I had no choice but to take her to a nursing home right next to the hospital. I assured her that it would only be temporary. I recall the last real conversation we had. She asked if I was truly happy and I told her that I'd never been happier. That seemed to satisfy her.

I know that she was greatly disappointed with my decision to leave the active ministry and asked me on a number of occasions if I thought the rules would change and the church would accept me back. At that time, shortly after Vatican II, I sincerely believed that celibacy would become optional and I'd soon be allowed to resume my duties as a priest.

A couple of nights after she was admitted to the nursing home, I stopped by to visit her after work. At first she seemed to be OK, and we talked a little bit about the care she was getting. Then I noticed a change. Her mind began to wander and she seemed frightened. She made me promise that I wouldn't leave her. I still didn't know how serious her condition was. The nurses helped her to the bathroom and when she returned to her bed, she started calling for her mother (who had been dead for many years). I panicked somewhat and went looking for her doctor, but he was unavailable, since he was involved in an emergency surgery.

I rushed back to her just in time to see one of the orderlies giving her mouth-to-mouth resuscitation. Then I heard one of the nurses say she was gone. At first, I couldn't believe it. I was totally confused, praying for her and calling her name. I asked for a phone and called a close priest friend who was in a nearby parish. He rushed over immediately and gave her the last rites.

It was over in such a short time that I thought I must be dreaming. I felt so guilty that I couldn't have done more. My mother was a very religious person and told me that a priest chaplain had been by a day or so earlier and had given her Communion. I knew that she was with God already, but I felt an emptiness that was only made worse with the realization that I hadn't really been close to her for several years and at times felt uncomfortable that she insisted on being wherever I was stationed as priest and chaplain. There were psychological reasons I've never been able to understand or explain, but I know that I loved her very much—and I also know that she knew it.

A couple days later, her doctor assured me that I had done all I could for her. Her heart was so enlarged that it had only been a matter of time. Even if he'd been able to tend to her that night and revive her, she still would have been gone within a few days.

I can only vaguely remember the hours and days that followed. I remember calling Jackie with the sad news. She'd left my father's home and was visiting with her mother in Wisconsin. She told me that she'd change her plane reservations that night and come back to Florida as quickly as possible. As in so many other instances, she was—and is—my strength. I walked most of the night, ending up at the beach with Linus. I was trying to clear my mind and think of what I must do.

Early the next morning, I called my father to tell him the news. I know it affected him very much, but we didn't talk long. Then I called George and we discussed their coming out for the funeral. I suggested that our mother be buried in Chicago rather than in Florida or Massachusetts (where her mother and some other members of the family were buried.) I didn't want her to be alone, but I had no idea how long we'd be in Florida, and most of her family was already gone. I knew George and Marilyn would never leave Chicago, so I wanted her to be there with them. George agreed and said with that in mind, that they wouldn't come to Florida. I'd have a funeral Mass for her in Florida and then she would be interred in Chicago, where they'd take care of all the arrangements.

Jackie and Jennifer returned and we had a funeral Mass a few days later. A few people from the institute attended. There was no one else nearby who could have come. Her only living brother and his wife in Milton, Massachusetts, might have come, but they were elderly and travel would have been difficult. Colonel Krise and the staff were very good to me. He told me to take as long as I needed before coming back to work.

George and I had little time to mourn our mother's death before we were plunged into more sadness. No sooner had our mother been buried than I had a call from Marion, telling me that our dad was very ill and not expected to live. The doctors at Ft. Belvoir Hospital were doing all they could, but his numerous illnesses were making it difficult for them to prescribe any antidotes to his latest condition— liver failure. Marion said that George was already on his way and would meet me at National Airport as soon as I could get a flight out. I told her I'd be there sometime that afternoon. George had been with our father all morning and told me that things looked very bad.

When I went in to see him, my father had just wakened. When a nurse told him I was there, he looked at me and I knew he recognized me. I can't remember much about what we said. I think he mentioned being glad to have seen and spent time with Jackie and his new granddaughter. I said he needed to hang on and get better, because Jennifer needed a grandfather.

Jennifer and my father, George

I remember his smiling a little and saying, "Yes, for awhile."

Then his voice drifted off and he fell asleep again.

Those were the last words I had with my father. I could only stay for a few days and then had to get back to work in Florida. Dad was in a coma when I left, and George said he was going to stay on for a few days. It was during that time that the doctors told Marion that his only hope of coming out of it was to operate, because he was bleeding internally.

Marion was too upset to make a decision, so she asked George to speak for her. After a lengthy discussion with the doctors, George gave the go-ahead to operate. He had little choice. I would have done the same thing. Dad didn't come out of the coma. They stopped the bleeding, but couldn't revive him. They said it would be over soon.

Marilyn and the boys came out from Chicago, and I brought Jackie and Jennifer. It must have been almost a week that we waited for any sign of consciousness, but it never came. The doctor said he couldn't predict how long Dad would linger in a comatose condition. With that in mind, George and I decided to return to our jobs and hoped that Marion could reach us in time.

**In front of George Senior's house: left to right,
Jim, Marion, George Jr., Jim, Mike, Tom, and Bob
(nephews), Marilyn, and baby Jennifer")**

I don't believe we were home more than two days when we received the call. Dad had died without regaining consciousness.

While my departure from Maryknoll was a bleak time in my life, nothing could compare with the emptiness I felt at the loss of both of my parents within the space of two weeks. We hadn't been a family for nearly thirty years, but my folks' separation affected me deeply. It may well have started me on a long, lonely road of depression that I've suffered, off and on, for the remainder of my life.

If I had depended upon my priesthood to get me through that awful period, I don't believe I would have made it. I needed a family—with shared love and a sense of mutual dependence. Jackie was the support that carried me through and gave me a reason for recovery. I wish that I could convey those thoughts to the Catholic hierarchy that has ostracized us and condemned us to absolute separation from our calling.

I believe that our God is a loving and forgiving God, but I also believe that He's a just God. At some point, I also believe that the obstinacy, fear, and revenge that bishops have seen fit to level against us must be answered for. There's no resemblance in their behavior to the mercy Jesus showed toward sinners and those marginalized by the leaders of His day.

George and I flew to Washington, without our families, for the funeral. Our father was laid to rest in Memorial Cemetery, less than a mile from where he and Marion had lived for the past thirty-five years. He had chosen not to be buried in Arlington National Cemetery, although he certainly deserved it. He had served in two World Wars and the Korean Conflict during nearly thirty years of military service. He wasn't quite sixty-nine years old at his death. My mother was seventy-six. They'd lived apart for more than thirty years, and yet, by the strangest of coincidences, they died within eighteen days of each other.

I was traumatized by everything that had happened so quickly. I felt sorrow, guilt, and loneliness. It was fortunate that I had Jackie and Jennifer to concentrate on, and my work to take my mind off my personal grief.

I wondered if perhaps I should seek the dispensation I had chosen not to request prior to our marriage. I suppose it was mainly because of my mother that I felt a need to apply. Jackie and I talked about it and she agreed that maybe it was the right thing to do, even though she had strong reservations. So I wrote to Rome for a dispensation from my promise to remain celibate for life. However, I included one caveat. I stated that I didn't believe that celibacy should be a mandatory part of becoming a priest.

Jim, Jackie, and Jennifer await the birth of second child

Initially, I had accepted that requirement, but after Vatican II, I could no longer believe that there was an essential connection between celibacy and priesthood. Little did I know then that a future pope (John Paul II) would publicly state the same thing—yet do nothing (during one of the longest papacies in history) to change the law.

Time passed. We learned in the summer of 1972 that we were going to be parents for a second time. On January 20, 1973, Jon Richard joined our family. We couldn't have been happier. Like most families, we spent as much time as possible with each other.

As I said earlier, the government made it possible for us to take our families when we made TDY trips by giving us ample funds and time to drive to most locations. That way, we could afford to take vacations in conjunction with work assignments.

Jim, Jackie, Jennifer(1 ½ years), and Jon (6 weeks)

After Jeffrey was born in 1974, I decided to make our Chevrolet Impala into a family traveling machine. The car was so wide that we could put all three kids in car seats in the backseat. I made a long shelf that fit across the back and fit into the door wells. I then made three compartments and lined them with kitchen shelf paper. Each child had their own space where they could read or play games and have their meals. (In retrospect, I think I should have patented it and made some money.)

It worked very well most of the time, except once when Jeff got car sick and upchucked his whole meal. Since he was in the middle, the other two made plenty of room for his disaster.

Our only venture in a motor home happened before Jeff was born. We rented one for a long weekend and drove from our home up to Daytona Beach, about ninety miles away. It was great fun, but a little too expensive for us to repeat. We were able to drive down onto the beach. Jennifer and Jon loved it and had a great time playing in the sand and making some cautious approaches to the surf. We cooked our meals in the motor home and avoided restaurants.

The three kids at Christmas 1975

After almost two years of waiting for an answer from Rome, we had given up any hope of hearing about my request. Then, one night I had a call from the priest who had come to anoint my mother. Since that time, we'd become good friends and saw him on a number of occasions. He told me that my dispensation had come through and he'd like to talk to me about it. He was working at the chancery in the marriage bureau. We were stunned. It had come without any warning, and we wondered how they had handled my rejection of celibacy.

We met the next day in my office at the base and read through the whole document as best we could. (As I recall, it was mostly in Latin.) The more we studied it, the worse we felt. First of all, Father told us that someone in the Orlando chancery office had informed Rome that I'd changed my mind about celibacy and recanted what I'd written in my letter requesting the dispensation. That's why it had come in such a hurry.

We had two concerns. First, they were granting it on the basis of false information. I hadn't changed my position. Second were the requirements I had to accept to receive the actual dispensation. I was to accept the possibility that I hadn't had the proper intention when I was ordained, so my ordination wasn't really valid. I was also urged to move away from the area and tell no one that I'd been a priest. Finally, I was to discontinue any contacts with priests I'd met in the area. All of it was meant to avoid giving scandal to the faithful. What hypocrites! If any scandal has been caused over the years, especially in light of the pedophile scandal, it has been given by the hierarchy.

Christmas in Florida, 1975

I don't blame any married priests who have left for their decision to accept a dispensation. I respect their decisions and only ask that they in turn respect mine. All our circumstances are different, and yet we've had one thing in common. The church leaders simply wanted us to vanish so they could wash their hands of us.

As one bishop stated publicly, "We've gotten rid of the bad ones. Now we'll have a purified priesthood."

For the most part, I enjoyed our time in Florida, despite the hot summers. Since there was no urgent need for Jackie to work outside the home, she was able to spend a great deal of time with our three children, and their physical, mental, and social progress reflected that.

Easter in Florida, 1976

My work at DRRI was enjoyable, and I found most of the staff and instructors accepting and supportive. It was also encouraging to know that we were having a positive effect on our military personnel by providing classes, seminars, group process, and inner city experience that gradually improved the racial and cultural atmosphere across the country and on overseas bases.

Then, however, the inevitable desire of the various services to have their own uniformed people in key positions at the institute became evident. We civilians all received notice that DOD was planning a

RIF, or reduction in force, at the institute. It wouldn't be immediate, but gradually all of us working in support positions would be replaced by senior enlisted people or officers, whether it took a few months or till the end of the year.

My turn came in August 1976, when I received a letter from DOD, telling me that my position would soon be abolished. The move was confirmed by the Director of DRRI, Colonel Robert Dews. I'd be forced to leave Florida and perhaps to return to Washington in order to find work at my same grade level. Fortunately, DRRI worked hard to help us find employment in the equal employment area, but before I discuss that aspect of our journey, I want to relate one incident I believe is important in understanding the human face of the institute.

My immediate supervisor, the senior education advisor at the institute, was a black PhD from the University of Pittsburgh. He'd come to the program with great expectations from the DRRI staff. In his first few months with the program, he made some radical changes in the curriculum, and faculty members were impressed. He and I got along well at first, but it was soon evident that he had very little respect for a white male in a race relations program.

Gradually, he made my life as miserable as possible and let it be known that I wasn't suitable for the job. During that time, another white male was hired. Fr. Leo Hahn (a priest, on leave of absence from his diocese) also had a PhD in Education and was hired as a psychologist. My boss was furious, since it became obvious that Leo's credentials far surpassed his own. He was determined to get rid of Leo, even though the faculty had great confidence in Leo's work.

He spread the word that Leo was a homosexual and an embarrassment to the institute. Ultimately, Leo left his position, returned to Colorado, and resumed his priestly duties. I mention that because it helps explain my boss' dislike for me. The animosity toward me accelerated to the point where we both agreed that we should meet with his boss (and mine), Colonel Dews, who was then Faculty Director (he later became director of the institute).

Colonel Dews was a man of great integrity. He was also black and had come up through the ranks during WWII. I had confidence that he'd look at the situation with the utmost fairness—and he did. When my boss had finished excoriating my behavior and recommended that I be terminated immediately, Colonel Dews calmly told him that he'd always respected his recommendations as Education Advisor, but in that instance, he didn't agree with him about my value to the institute. He wouldn't terminate my employment, but the colonel would move me from under his supervision and make me the head of a new branch, Tests and Measurements, reporting directly to him for my assignments.

I was deeply grateful to Colonel Dews for his fairness and confidence. (He ultimately retired from the Army as a full colonel and joined the Peace Corps).

CHAPTER TEN

A NEW OPPORTUNITY

We left Florida and the institute with some trepidation. I wasn't receiving a transfer. I was actually out of work and had to go through a whole new process of job hunting. Nothing was guaranteed, and it all depended on the Navy to decide if I had the qualifications to be hired in another new program called Shore Equal Opportunity Program (SEOP), an Equal Opportunity program that had grown out of the DRRI experience, but totally Navy.

SEOP was intended to brief Navy commands in the U.S. and abroad about the DOD's commitment to fair and impartial treatment of all its employees worldwide. Once again, it would be civilians, in teams of two, who would do the briefing—sometimes to a hostile command structure that wasn't sympathetic to the military racial awareness program. Many of the top brass felt that the DOD had become too proactive in that area. The Navy had its own idea as to how to handle diversity, and it wasn't with kid gloves.

While living in the D.C./Virginia area during the next period of our journey, we either owned or rented six homes from 1977–84. I had several interviews with the Navy EEO people before being hired as an EEO Specialist. At the same time, I was interviewing elsewhere, just to keep my options open. It was during those other interviews that I met someone working in the Alcohol Prevention division of the National Health Institute (NIH).

This contact was kind enough to meet with me, but had to caution me that there weren't many openings in the NIH at that time. In fact, he was on his way out of government. He and his wife, were contemplating a move to Maine where they hoped to start a new life as owners and operators of a bed-and-breakfast. I wished him well and thanked him for meeting with me. Little did I know that I'd meet them again, some years later under very different circumstances.

During my waiting period to be hired, we happened on a group of Catholics who were meeting weekly for Mass at a school auditorium in northern Virginia. They had the interesting label of the Nova Group. The group, numbering about seventy-five families, was made up mostly of disaffected parishioners from several parishes. Most were professionals: lawyers, doctors, teachers, and government workers. There were many children in attendance and a great deal of attention was given to them and their spiritual development. That was thirty years ago and there were no active married priests to speak of, so they invited religious order priests teaching at Catholic University, Georgetown, and other Catholic colleges in the area to offer Mass for the group.

Initially, the institutional church was opposed to the group, but when we became participants, there seemed to be little opposition. They tried not to call too much attention to themselves and went about quietly practicing their faith. So far as I know, the group still exists, but we've long since lost touch with the leadership.

The involvement with Nova was something we really needed at the time. There were other married priests and their families who belonged to the group, but none, to our knowledge, were administering the Sacraments or officiating at marriages. Our children were still preteens at that time. They liked Nova and its informality and acceptance of everyone who came to worship. Jennifer and Jon both made their First Communion at Nova and prized the little wooden crosses the community gave them with their names and date of Communion inscribed. It was a good period of spiritual formation for them—and for us, as well.

We also came into touch with another smaller group called the Sunday Bunch. Many were married priests and many of the women were former nuns. Long after our departure from the Washington area, we retained friendship with Carl and Pat Hemmer and Joe and Kathy Kerns. Carl and Joe were both former Jesuits. Joe Kerns passed away a few years ago, but Jackie still stays in touch with Kathy by phone on special memorial days. Our children were older when we discovered the Sunday Bunch and they felt very close to the eight or ten couples who met as frequently as possible. We'd have the liturgy together and then a potluck dinner while continuing our discussion for several hours. It was a special group, and I believe it helped us during that time in our lives to keep our faith despite the church institution's rejection.

Reunion of the 'Sunday Bunch'

Jackie mentioned not long ago that Jon, in recent years, told her on one occasion that while he didn't always understand the very deep theological insights in Joe Kerns' sermons, he was always impressed that over dinner Joe would happily discuss football and other interests with him. Joe, I think, was the grandfather the children really never had, since both Jackie's and my dad had died before the boys were born and Jennifer was just an infant when Jackie brought her to see Grandpa Lovejoy in 1972.

Fortunately, we didn't have to wait as long for my second job to materialize. The folks at DRRI had given us all good recommendations, and the Navy EEO office wasted little time in bringing us on for the SEOP program. Though we enjoyed the warm winters and time at the beach while we lived in Florida, I think we were happy to be further north and to experience the changing of the seasons.

My first assignment with the Navy was at Naval Material Command in Crystal City, Arlington, Virginia. There we helped put together a curriculum that SEOP would introduce to the Navy's command structure. A young black woman and I were assigned to work at headquarters as coordinators of the program while some ten two-person teams were assigned to different parts of the continental United States to present the EEO program to each Navy command in their geographical area.

Jackie and I were both very fond of my colleague, and I remember one occasion when we double dated with her and a boyfriend at the Wolf Trap open air theater to hear Henry Mancini in concert. We had a delicious lunch and watched the event from a grassy knoll overlooking the theater. Jackie had planned the event to celebrate my fiftieth birthday. (My wife and I also went to see *Carousel* there a few years later.)

Shortly after arriving in Virginia, we took a ride with the children out to an area called Bushy Ridge, almost at the West Virginia line. We'd heard that there were some lots for sale, some with rustic camps, on the site. We were so impressed with the quiet solitude that we decided to purchase a simple A-frame on one of the lots, as a getaway from the city.

It was quite a distance from our home, so we could only make occasional trips there. On one of those trips, we had a near disaster. Jackie and I were getting dinner ready in the house, while all three children went exploring. All of a sudden, we heard blood-curdling screams coming from a grove not far away. As I ran out the back door, I saw the kids running madly toward the house, waving their hands and slapping at their bodies.

Jim and the kids at Bushy Ridge, Virginia

They had stumbled into a hive of bees, and the bees were swarming around them as they ran up the hill. I ran down to meet them and grabbed Jeff, who was the youngest, and we all lit out for the A-frame. Jackie was frantically trying to find something to soothe the stings. Fortunately, none of the children were allergic to bee stings, so they didn't begin to swell, but they were petrified and couldn't stop crying. They had all been stung several times. One of them had been stung on the nose and it was swelling somewhat, while another had gotten stung right on the buttocks, which we all laughed about later—but not at that time.

We had only ice cubes to use at first, but then drove to a drug store, where we were able to get some ointment. It wasn't long after that incident that we decided the A-frame and the remote location hadn't been my greatest idea after all, so we sold the property.

However, that venture wasn't a complete disaster, since during our travels there we had come upon a property near the Blue Ridge Mountains and Front Royal, Virginia, that was for sale as a permanent home. We knew that it would be a long drive for me (fifty-five miles), but we thought it would be worth it to have a beautiful home in that area to enjoy country living. The home at Linden, Virginia, was perched atop a mountain in Skyline Estates.

A visit to Gloucester and "Captain Courageous"

The owner, who had worked in the space program, had an illness that necessitated his living near Washington and his doctors, so he was willing to sell at a price within our range. We moved there in October 1978. Jennifer was almost seven, Jon was five, and Jeff was four, so only Jennifer was in school. We lived in that home until June 1981.

Jackie had the responsibility for getting them all off to school every morning. The school bus only came part way up the mountain, so she had to take them down to the bus every day, sometimes walking them down in winter when it was too icy to drive.

I was off to work at 5:30 a.m. so I could make it into work by 7:30, flex-time. Believe it or not, I rode in a car pool with other people as crazy as we were who chose to live in that remote region. Despite the drawbacks, we loved it there, enjoyed our weekends of solitude, and I spent more time with the children there than elsewhere. They were still young enough to play together and although they made some friends on the mountain and in town (Front Royal), most of their play time was with each other. I remember especially the safaris we'd take, pretending we were making long trips through the woods. Jackie would make us all lunches and we'd set out on one adventure after another.

We didn't have many visitors to our mountaintop home, but I remember the time Jackie's friend Barbara, from Milwaukee, came to visit with her husband, Cal, in a large motor home. It was quite a project getting that huge vehicle up the mountain and then down the steep hill to our home, which was built into the side of the mountain. It took some real maneuvering, but Cal managed to make it into our circular driveway. The kids enjoyed their visit and the wonderful meals that Barbara insisted on cooking for us.

In 1981, we left Skyline Estates and headed back to Washington. My job had changed for the Navy. I was working for Chief of Naval Operations, but still in the EEO offices. We were housed in large barracks, built during World War II to supplement the Pentagon. (They were the offices for Navy personnel and the headquarters of the Marine Corps at that time.) My new job was to coordinate and update the Navy's EEO discrimination complaint policy.

I enjoyed the work initially, but after several years I began to feel cooped up in my small office cubicle. I communicated mostly by phone with commands around the country and overseas. However, I had little real interaction with people other than the staff. I was getting restless and somewhat depressed, and Jackie could see it.

She used to say, "Jim could die at the Pentagon and no one would ever know it."

She was referring to the ambulances that would occasionally arrive at the Pentagon near my place of work and cart someone off who'd had a heart attack—or something worse. So we began to discuss my leaving government work—but what would we do? I had a good paying job and a very young family to support. We couldn't just retire.

Because of our background in religion and social work, we thought we might look into some kind of social service—maybe in geriatrics—but we'd need further education to qualify for that sort of work. Then I thought of the NIH employee and his plan to start a bed-and-breakfast in Maine with his wife. We managed to locate them and discovered that he *had* left government service. Then they'd purchased an old vacant building and converted it to a combination restaurant and lodge called Pilgrim's Inn, located in Deer Isle, Maine, a small fishing village in the Downeast area. So began a new chapter in our lives.

Our family portrait the year we move to Maine

In the summer of 1982, our family made an extensive trip to New England with a pop-up camper. It was our first exploratory excursion to find a location and a place of business. We traveled through Vermont and New Hampshire, where we stayed at a family campground and in a large motel. We considered both of those places as possible work sites, but dismissed them because of the investment involved. We finally arrived in Maine and camped at Pemaquid Point, where we cooked lobsters and clams for a wonderful seafood feast. It was during that visit that we decided our new home would be in Maine.

The following year, Jackie and I made a similar trip by ourselves and ended up in Downeast Maine, where we visited our friends, the B&B owners. They had sold Pilgrim's Inn and purchased a resort called The End of the Beyond. It consisted of a main house and cabins on several acres overlooking a secluded river opening out to the ocean in Sunset, near Deer Isle. We stayed with them a couple nights and picked their brains about starting a similar business. We didn't want anything so elaborate or involved. We just wanted to open a bed-and-breakfast as a family business. They gave us some ideas and wished us well.

For the next six months, we took all the leave I could muster from the Navy and drove to Maine four or five times to look for property. We knew we wanted to be on or near the ocean and that we needed a place large enough to house at least a dozen guests.

Finally, in January 1984, we found a place we liked that was for sale in *DownEast* magazine. It was located in Belfast, in the Midcoast part of Maine, about 150 miles north of Kittery. We remembered that we'd stopped in Belfast for coffee on one of our trips, but it hadn't impressed us, probably because it was in the late fall on a foggy, dreary day. We contacted the realtor and arranged to drive up from Virginia the following weekend.

We arrived at the appointed time, but to our dismay, the owners had decided to take the property off the market. (That was before the days of cell phones, so the realtor couldn't be blamed for failing to contact us along the way.) Needless to say, we were exhausted and disappointed.

The realtor offered to show us other places for sale in the area, and we felt duty-bound to at least take a look. We spent the remainder of the afternoon looking at one place after another. They were either too small, too expensive, or not in the right location. Finally, we thanked her and said we'd be heading home the next day.

She told us, "Well, I've been saving this one until last. It's a good buy and about the size you need, but it *does* need work."

We were to find out that when someone in Maine says a place needs work, they're not exaggerating.

We said, "Well, where is it?"

We'd just finished looking at the next-to-last house on her list, and she said, "Just turn around and look across the street."

We weren't prepared for the sight we beheld, and I just groaned—but there it was, 19 Church St., a big Greek Revival home, vintage 1840, on almost an acre of land in the heart of Belfast's historic section. We didn't know whether to laugh or cry. The place was overrun with weeds and a high, untrimmed hedge. The white house almost looked gray from lack of paint, and any paint that was left was peeling everywhere.

We went to the back door, where two pillars were hanging unattached to the floorboards. A barn and a carriage house were attached to the house. It wasn't until we entered the house and made our way through the maze of boxes and assorted articles (a family was living there temporarily) and began to look at the amazing appointments that our disappointment began to turn to awe and hope.

There were five marble fireplaces in the house, and a cherry wood mantel in the master bedroom upstairs. There was a nicely carved cherry staircase in immaculate condition, a walk-in china closet in the dining room, and a pocket door leading to the front hall. Those were just a few of the charming features we saw during our tour of the house.

When we returned to Virginia, we carefully analyzed our potential move because it was a big decision. We'd seen the house and knew that converting it to a bed-and-breakfast would be a formidable task. We knew nothing about providing services to guests, and we knew even less about the challenge of turning a huge 150-year-old home into a comfortable place for people to stay on their vacations.

My stepmother had died shortly before our contemplated move, and my brother and I knew that we'd be receiving an inheritance from my father's estate, but we didn't know how much or how long it would take to go through probate court. Jackie and I had some money to work with, because I'd taken my thirteen years of government retirement in a lump sum, but how long would that last?

We discussed our plans with the children, but they were still too young to understand the implications. I'm sure they had some anxiety about moving away from their friends and familiar surroundings, but none of them voiced any strong reactions. They seemed to be excited about moving to Maine and starting a business of our own.

I was fifty-five years old at the time and Jackie was forty-six. Most people would have been looking ahead to retirement in less than ten years, but we were about to enter a brand new field without any assurance that we'd be successful.

In a way, we were burning some bridges behind us. I had serious responsibilities to Jackie and to our children (age 12, 10, and 9), and I was severing my ties with government service. I was becoming disenchanted with federal service and really wanted to be my own boss. We felt that the children would be better served by moving to a small rural community, where class sizes would allow them to more easily get to know all of their classmates. However, we also knew that if we were making a mistake with the move, it would be very difficult to find comparable employment at my age—especially in Maine.

Chapter Eleven
Only with Risks Can True Happiness Come!

Amid all the doubts and misgivings, we decided to go ahead with our plans. On the day we called the realtor in Belfast, she told us that there was a back-up contract on the property and that we should probably offer to pay the $65,000 asking price on the house if we'd really decided to go ahead with the purchase. Within a few days she called back and told us that the owners had accepted our offer, with certain conditions. (Later, we learned that the other offer had been only $5,000 less.)

We were very excited, and now that we'd made the decision, we knew that we could handle it and that we'd eventually have a successful business. We set the closing date for the house in April. Then we'd rent a twenty-four-foot U-Haul to ship our belongings. I'd drive the truck and Jackie would follow in our Volare. The children would take turns riding with me and their mother. We thought it would take us two days to drive from Virginia to Maine.

When I told my car pool members that we were moving to Maine to own and operate a bed-and-breakfast, they thought I was crazy. One of them, who worked for the Army at the Pentagon and was counting the days until his retirement and his move south to Florida, seriously counseled me about such a drastic move.

He said, "Don't you know that come November, that whole area is frozen tundra?"

I just smiled, since I knew that he'd never even traveled north of Virginia. I assured him that I had lived in the north most of my life and that things weren't really that bad—even in January!

We agreed upon April 10, 1984 as our closing date, so we had less than three months to terminate my work with the government, pack all of our possessions, and move to Maine. I worked out an arrangement with the Navy to use all of my sick leave and then be terminated. That would give us time to make the move and get settled in.

After a rather hectic trip, during which the Volare conked out, causing us to have to replace some parts, we finally reached Belfast shortly before our scheduled closing date. I drove the U-Haul into the parking area of our future home and left it there while we all piled into the Volare and headed downtown to the lawyer's office. The realtor suggested that we leave the children at the library during the closing. Fortunately, our kids liked to read so they were satisfied with that plan. Little did we know that the closing would take almost four hours.

I thought we could have been finished in half that time, but the seller turned out to be a real jerk. He was ridiculous, arguing over every point that came up. We kept conceding, and he kept insisting on more conditions. Finally, I told both realtors and the lawyer to just get it settled and let us get on with our lives. We were all exhausted after our trip from Virginia, and I knew that the kids were probably starving.

When the signing was finally over, Jackie and I dashed to the library to rescue Jennifer and the boys. They were somewhat satisfied when I told them that the realtor who had the contract, George Jennings, had invited us all to join him and his wife for dinner at a nice seafood restaurant. George was a great guy. He'd been a sea captain and really looked the part. In fact, everyone called him Captain Jennings. I got to know George over the years and he became a good and loyal friend. His wife was also very nice and apologized for the client who'd been such a boor about the sale.

After a wonderful dinner, all we wanted to do was get back to the house and get some sleep. We brought in only what we needed and slept on mattresses that we spread out on the floor.

The days ahead would be busy. We needed to unpack the U-Haul, get settled in, and start working on the house to make it suitable for the guests we hoped to have in a few months when the tourist season got underway. We didn't have the luxury of some bed-and-breakfast owners who came after us and spent their first full year refurbishing their places. We needed an income as soon as possible.

One thing I had drilled into our children was that we'd *chosen* to go to Maine and to that town. No one had asked us to come, so it was up to us to fit in. I asked them not to start telling new friends at school about the wonderful advantages they'd had in Virginia. The locals were proud of their town, and it was up to us to see how well we could fit in as newcomers. If people asked about our former home and schools, we would tell them, but not in a bragging way. The kids heeded my advice and were well accepted by those they got to know.

Jeff was in fourth grade, so he'd finish out the year at Pierce Grade School. Jon was in the sixth grade, so he enrolled at Robertson School, and Jennifer just walked down Church Street to the middle school, since she was in the seventh grade.

We were later to learn that Crosby School had formerly been Belfast's high school, and back in the mid-fifties, it had been prominently depicted in a movie (quite risqué at that time) called *Peyton Place*. It was about scandals that took place in a small New England town and was one of Hollywood's early attempts to discuss marital infidelity. Some folks who lived in Belfast at that time served as extras in the film—that is, if their parents approved!

Belfast is a town of approximately 6,500. That was part of the reason why we left Virginia. We wanted our children to grow up in small town America, where we felt they'd have a better chance of getting to know their classmates and of doing better academically, in sports, and in other activities.

Belfast has two newspapers, the *Republican Journal*, which dated back to the early twentieth century, and the *Waldo Independent*, which broke off from the *Journal* while we were living in Belfast. Both papers flourished. The *Journal* used to have a picture each week of a place in the area, and readers were invited to write in and try to guess where it was. Shortly after we moved into our home, a photographer took a picture of a part of our house's peeling paint, which made it hard to recognize. I don't remember if anyone guessed the location correctly or not.

Before we had the house scraped and painted, it looked pretty awful—so bad, in fact, that Jennifer was ashamed to tell her new school friends where she lived. She'd walk right by the house and up the street a ways, and told her friends that she lived on some other street. (She only told us about that much later). I couldn't say that I blamed her. However, once the house was painted and fixed up, I think they were all proud to say that it was their home.

We lived in Belfast for almost thirteen years, from 1984–96. We operated our bed-and-breakfast for all of those years, and although we never got rich, I think it was a good experience for all of us. It helped us stay in touch with people from all over the world, and many of them came back for return visits.

During the early days, when we really didn't know where the money would come from to work on the inn, I fell into a deep depression and confessed to Jackie that I felt as if we'd made a mistake. I suggested that maybe we should try to sell the house and return to Virginia in the hope that I could get my job back with the government.

It was a difficult time for Jackie. She was more determined than ever to make a go of it, although it had really been my idea. She insisted that we could make it and did her best to lift my spirits. I finally had to get psychological help and started taking medication to relieve my depression. At first I didn't believe anything would help, but I gradually began to show some improvement.

We met a couple about our age who lived a few streets away in an old broken-down building, but the husband was a good carpenter and volunteered his time to help us get on our feet. His wife convinced Jackie to start on one room at a time.

As she said, "Just clean one room at a time and you'll see how much easier it is to do the others."

She was right, and we were able to fix up enough rooms to be able to open our doors to guests on June 1, 1984.

The Hiram Alden Inn – Our family owned Bed and Breakfast from 1984 – 1996 in Belfast, Maine

I don't think we'll ever forget our first guests—a friendly young couple with a large black dog. The dog was perfectly disciplined and they assured us that he wouldn't damage the house if we let him sleep in their room. Our success with those first guests made us realize that we could do it, and that people would be satisfied with the hospitality we offered. That's not to say that we didn't have disappointments or have to make changes in our approach, but at least we knew that our new way of life hadn't been a mistake. Our success with the hundreds of travelers who stayed with us over the next several years encouraged us to stick with it, even when we were tempted to question our ability as innkeepers.

One day when Jennifer was helping me with a sign she'd painted advertising our inn, a couple came by and talked with us. Their names are Mary and Aimee Proulx, and they attended our church up the street, St. Francis.

Mary asked Jennifer what grade she was in, and when Jennifer told her, she said, "Oh, so you'll be in my class next year! That's nice!"

We've remained good friends with that couple, even though we moved away in 1996. They were the first ones to call us on the morning a story was published in the paper telling of my work as a married priest and of Jackie's support. Although they are devout Catholics, they said they believed it was right for me to provide service to those who were unwilling or unable to practice their faith in the institutional church. They also believed strongly in the need for a married priesthood.

Both Jackie and I tried to provide service to our community whenever the demands of the inn would allow it. Jackie substituted as a teacher at all levels of education. She also offered her services in many ways to organizations and individuals. I served as Executive Director of the Chamber of Commerce for ten years and served one term on the city council. We were both active with sports teams, because all three of our children played a number of sports.

I remember one amusing incident shortly after we had arrived in the town. Both boys played on the same Little League team, so we were fixtures at just about every game that first summer. One of Jeff's friends commented to him that he thought it was great that his grandfather came to every game.

Jeff looked at him for a moment and then blurted out, "That's not my grandfather. That is my father!"

I was a little taken aback when Jeff told me, but then reminded myself that I was fifty-six years old, and most of the other team member's grandfathers were probably just about that age!

That first year, we realized that we'd need more income than we could earn from the inn if we were going to make it, so I called the people I'd worked for in the Navy and asked if there were any open positions as a part-time Equal Employment Opportunity Deputy in the area. There was an opening. I applied and was hired.

The only problem was that I had to travel every week to Groton, Connecticut. I did that for about six months until the winter came and I knew that I couldn't keep it up. However, by that time the inheritance from my father's estate had become available, making it possible for us to put our full energy into the operation and repair of the inn.

We stayed open all year, hoping that we'd have guests over the holiday period, but they were infrequent, since we were on the coast and not in a ski or snowmobile area. At any rate, it was during the winter that we were able to do most of our work on the building—and it needed an enormous amount of work!

Those thirteen years of service as innkeepers seemed to fly by. As the children grew older, they were a great help in our maintaining the property. Both boys got some great experience in house painting and repairs, which helped Jeff in later years, since he later painted houses in the summer while being employed as a teacher during the school year. Jon went on to work for a leading home builder in Atlanta, and his experience at the inn and working with local carpenters, as well as two years of architecture at Syracuse University, stood him in good stead when he applied for a position with John Weilland Homes.

Jennifer's artistic ability was evident from her earliest years. She painted the Hiram Alden Inn sign in the front yard for us at the age of twelve. We had our roof redone the second year, and she painted on many of the slates that were left over, selling hundreds of them at the inn and at city fairs. My favorite one, a painting of a red barn on the way to Winterport, still hangs in our living room. We also have a beautiful depiction of the inn after it had been repainted.

In my office in Kennebunk, just below a fifty-year-old picture of my mother and Uncle Rob receiving Holy Communion from me at my first Solemn High Mass at St. Mary's parish in Lynn, Massachusetts, there is one of Jennifer's most memorable slates, entitled "Children Do Not Realize."

Jackie and I treasure that slate, because it's really a tribute to our three children:

Children do not realize
Until the years have flown
How thoughtful are their parents' ways,
How very much their own,
How loving
Are their parents' hearts,
How deep is their concern
How many special things they do
With no thought of return
But by and by, they come to see
And realize their worth,
And know for sure their parents
Are their dearest friends
On Earth!

Would that our Catholic hierarchy, whose contempt for our marriages as priests has hardened their hearts for the many years since our departure from their ranks, could understand the depth of love between our spouses and ourselves and the children many of us have brought into this world and who love and serve God in their own individual ways. No one other than those mitered bachelors has ever accused me of scandal, but countless good Catholic people have come to see where the real scandal lies—in the intent and actions of the hierarchy!

No matter how busy we were at the inn during the summer months, Jackie would insist that the boys and I take off for at least a few days and go camping so we could have some quality time together. Since we lived on the Atlantic coast, we'd travel across the state to campsites on the western lakes. Our favorite spot was Rangeley Lake. We did that for three summers, until the boys were old enough to attend camp with some of their friends. I have to admit that my intentions were good, but each summer I was less enthusiastic about sleeping on a bedroll on the hard ground.

The first summer, we slept in tents and really roughed it. The boys loved it. The second summer, we stayed in a makeshift cabin on beds with springs. The last summer, at my suggestion, we rented a condo and slept on real beds. That was the summer I realized that the boys weren't kids anymore and were growing up. We had rented a small boat with an outboard motor, and they constantly fought over which of them should operate the tiller.

Then one day, Jon asked, "Dad, could Jeff and I take a spin ourselves? We'll be careful and be back in a half hour."

I knew that their mother wouldn't have approved, even though Jon was thirteen and both of them were excellent swimmers, but I reluctantly gave my permission. However, when a half hour had passed and they hadn't returned, I began to worry. When they had been gone an hour, I began to panic. Then I heard the motor and saw them rounding the bend and heading for our campsite. I scolded them a bit for staying out too long and asked if they'd gotten lost.

"No," they replied in unison, "we were on our way back, but some girls waved at us from the shore and we thought we should be polite and stop to see what they wanted."

"So," I said in mock anger, "what did they want?"

"They just wanted to be friendly," Jeff said with a sly smile.

At the end of our first summer, we needed to go somewhere for the day, so right after Labor Day, the whole family drove up to Acadia National Park, near Bar Harbor, Maine. We spent the day there and although it was a bit cool, we drove to Sandy Beach (which is one of only a few real sandy beaches north of Old Orchard). The boys wanted to go swimming, even though there were tourists gathered about in sweaters and light jackets.

The next thing I knew, they were running down the beach and diving into the cold fall water. Jackie and I stood there shivering and watching them. A couple of ladies standing near us commented on what they saw. They couldn't believe that Jeff and Jon were actually in the water, swimming as though they were in Florida.

One lady said to the other, "Well, they must be native Mainers! Who else would be crazy enough to swim in those waters at this time of year?"

Jackie just smiled, first at me, and then at Jennifer.

Later, as we were leaving, those same ladies looked on in astonishment and asked where we were from.

Jackie smiled and said, "They were both born in Florida and we've just moved here from Virginia."

I heard a gasp and an "I don't believe it" as we walked past them to the car.

When I took over the Chamber of Commerce as its executive director, the Chamber was almost inactive. I volunteered to take it over on one condition: that I receive $16,000 the first year, and if we built it up sufficiently during that year, I'd receive $20,000 the second and all succeeding years. The board of directors agreed and we set out to revitalize the membership. I made a lot of friends among the local businesspeople the following ten years and had a staff of about fifteen volunteers to keep the Chamber office open year round.

We moved into a building near the waterfront that was owned by Phil Rackliffe, a retired local funeral director. We rented the large front room as a display area and kept a room in back for my office and that of a secretary we'd hired. Phil had living quarters in an attached building that looked out over the bay. We became fast friends and enjoyed each other's company immensely.

Phil was a Belfast native and loved to tell wild stories about the early days when Belfast wasn't so gentrified. He'd quit smoking in recent years, but not soon enough. He had an advanced case of emphysema and after he had returned to Arizona (where he spent the winters) one fall, we learned of his death at the age of seventy.

Phil had a favorite expression that he always came back with whenever anyone asked how he was doing.

He'd smile broadly and with a twinkle in his eye, he'd say in a loud voice, "Just elegant!"

He'd use that phrase even as he walked out of his quarters with tubes in his nose, dragging a tank of oxygen behind him.

Phil liked our Jennifer. He thought that she was an enterprising young lady and he admired one of her art projects, a large map of Belfast that she'd painted on the wall of the town bathhouse. It faced the roadway leading down to the dock from the stores on Main Street and our little railroad, the Belfast and Moosehead Lake Railroad, which had once been a thriving freight operation but with the demise of most of the industry had become a popular tourist run.

One of my favorite memories of the railroad was the time we brought a group of Japanese businessmen and government officials into town. Those very staid businesspeople, in suits and ties, soon put aside their attire and then, in shirtsleeves and open collars, joined in group singing and dancing—and even good-naturedly let themselves be taken as hostages during a pretend holdup by masked bandits. We fed them baked beans and hot dogs, which they eagerly devoured. (It was only afterward that we found out that Japanese abhor baked beans!)

Jackie became involved with our local parish. Her beautiful singing voice was discovered by many when she sang the national anthem at a number of sporting events, and despite our estrangement from the church, the local Catholic pastor recruited Jackie as choir director for St. Francis' excellent adult choir. Together with Barbara Marsanskis, a wonderful lady and the parish organist, Jackie provided the leadership needed for that group. Barbara has remained a good friend through the years and an avid supporter of the married priesthood.

Jackie also helped prepare young adults of the parish for Confirmation, and she was called upon many times to substitute teach at all levels in the schools—and even did a stint on the local school board.

We have many good memories of our years in Belfast. Although we've been gone for more than ten years, we still have strong ties to that community. Not long ago, I was invited to offer Mass for members of the Voice of the Faithful at one of their homes, and I was asked to participate actively in the memorial service for another dear friend, Linus Heinz, by his wife, Pat, who asked me to carry the Franciscan San Damiano Cross into St. Francis Catholic Church. Linus and Pat were dear friends who we came to know and respect as Innkeepers and colleagues. Jackie and I have stayed in touch with Pat and will happily continue to do so.

One Valentine's Day, a reporter for the *Republican Journal* asked if we'd be willing to be interviewed for a piece they were doing. He knew that I'd left the active ministry to marry, and asked if we'd mind telling the story of how we'd met and subsequently married many years ago. We thought about it and accepted the offer.

The article included our journey and that of several other couples, but I'm sure that our story drew the most attention. Most residents of Belfast hadn't known much about our past. We were besieged with phone calls and meetings on the street and in shopping areas. As I recall, there wasn't one critical remark from anyone, even the most devout Catholics.

Most people said essentially the same thing: "We saw the article about you and Jackie, and we're so happy to know this about you. We believe that the church should welcome married priests back into active ministry."

Those comments were made long before the scandalous events of the past few years, involving pedophile priests and cover-ups by their bishops.

Since our tourist season was relatively brief (June–October) and we didn't draw patrons during the winter due to the lack of snow along the coast, we didn't enjoy a very lucrative income from the bed-and-breakfast operation alone. We had to supplement our income with my work with the Chamber of Commerce and Jackie's substitute teaching. However, we managed to get by and feed our family.

The real benefit of inn-keeping was the opportunity to meet people from all over the world. We had guests from all over Europe, from Latin America, Australia, Japan, Africa, China, and India, as well as folks traveling in the States. Our prices were somewhat lower than other bed-and-breakfasts in Belfast because we'd decided to run our inn on the European model, with shared baths. Over time, the more affluent bed-and-breakfasts were able to capture a good part of the market, but we persevered and lasted longer than most.

Jennifer entered college and the boys would soon follow, but when we decided to leave Belfast, we found it difficult to sell our property. There was a limited market in the 1990s for such enterprises. Unlike our experience of purchasing the Hiram Alden Inn for $65,000 in 1984, the average inn was selling at that time for $200,000 to $300,000, and there weren't many takers.

In June 1996, I had a falling out with members of the Chamber's board over certain issues with which I couldn't agree. I resigned my position and entered into an agreement with some folks interested in establishing a countywide Chamber. I set up an office in Unity, Maine (about twenty-five miles west of Belfast) and began an intense recruiting effort to organize county businesses.

That fall, we found a buyer for the inn, and in September we moved to Unity. Within a year, I'd recruited more businesses for the Waldo County Chamber than there were in the Belfast organization. I was happy with our progress and felt that in another year, the new Chamber would be self-sustaining. However, in December 1997, I was disappointed when those who had agreed to financially support the new endeavor pulled the plug and discontinued my salary.

For the next five years, I worked as a consultant to a tourist marketing organization out of Tallahassee, Florida. They sent representatives from their headquarters to promote Waldo County as a tourist destination. Jackie and I got to know the president of the company, very well and she was good to us during that time. Unfortunately, the disaster of 9-11 had a serious financial impact on their work and they were forced to cut back.

My work with that marketing company ended in March 2002, so we had to reevaluate our situation and decide what we could do to make a living. It was a difficult time for us. The only consolation was that our children had all gone through college and had begun careers of their own. As in the past, we held firmly to our philosophy that as one door closed, God would open another one for us to enter.

Opening another door to our future

CHAPTER TWELVE
THE PEOPLE NEED ME AND I NEED THEM!

I have a little cartoon taped to my office wall. It's a sketch of a large pelican standing in marshy waters with a frog that he's about to swallow. However, the frog has his hands held tightly around the pelican's neck, choking him so that he can't swallow.

The caption under the picture says it all: "Never give up!"

That's always been our motto! We've been in some tight situations, but somehow we've always found a way to keep going—and I'll give much of the credit to Jackie. She has an indomitable spirit and whenever I'm tempted to throw in the towel, she always convinces me that we can work it out—and we always do.

One day, we visited a good friend, a retired Catholic priest, who lives in Bar Harbor and a few years my senior. I told him that I wanted to do something to help Catholics who had become disenchanted with the church and needed spiritual help. He introduced us to a group of married priests and their wives in Portland, Maine. He thought it would help if we could talk about our concerns with others who had left the active ministry but had remained Catholics.

A few weeks after our visit with this priest, we contacted the organizers of that small group. They were delighted with our call and invited us to attend their next meeting, which was to be held at their Portland home. There were five or six couples at that meeting, and they all welcomed us warmly. We had a spiritual service with songs and readings, but not a Mass, as I recall.

After the service we had lunch, consisting of dishes brought to the meeting by each couple, and then we spent time discussing the readings and socializing.

It was at that meeting that I said I wanted to become active again as a married priest. Although only a couple of the married priests there were carrying on a ministry (particularly weddings), they all encouraged me to look into the possibility. One of them gave me a small pamphlet he'd been given by a representative of a married priests group that was very active in ministering to Catholics and others who for one reason or another either couldn't or chose not to participate in the institutional church.

I wasn't impressed with the title of the pamphlet. It seemed too commercialized at the time. However, I glanced through it and put it in my coat pocket to read later. Its title was *Rent-a-Priest*.

It was not until the next day that I happened to reach into my pocket and found the pamphlet, and Jackie and I both read it. We were especially impressed with the church canons (laws) that supported a married priesthood. (Naturally, the institution wouldn't have agreed and would have given a much different interpretation of those canons.) We also learned that the official name for the group was CITI—not to be confused with the mega-bank that uses the same initials. The group's initials stand for "Celibacy is the Issue."

There was a number to call for additional information, so I called and talked to a lady by the name of Louise Haggett. She explained the information in the pamphlet in more detail and how she, a devout practicing Catholic, had become the spearhead for the organization of a married priest group dedicated to providing service when and wherever needed—as validly ordained Catholic priests.

Louise told me how she had tried to find a priest to anoint her dying mother in a nursing home and simply couldn't find one who could come at that moment. She had been astounded at the shortage of priests, even some twelve years ago. She immediately contacted two married priests she knew and told them that something had to be done. Out of this meeting came Rent-a-Priest—calling resigned priests, most of whom were married, to a renewal of their ministry.

Most Catholics are amazed when you tell them that more than 25,000 validly ordained Roman Catholic priests left the active ministry from the end of Vatican Council II (in 1965) until recently—enough priests to fill the vacuum that's now evident throughout the country. If those priests would be allowed to return, every Catholic parish in the United States would once again have its own pastor—in one stroke of a pen by the pope.

The pope has it in his power to remove the mandatory requirement of celibacy for the ordination of priests, because as was mentioned earlier, there's no essential connection between celibacy and priesthood.

I told Louise that I wanted to join the group immediately. She asked me to send my credentials of ordination to Framingham, Massachusetts, where the CITI archives were located.

This is about the time that Jackie and I were planning a special adventure. To celebrate our 30th anniversary in January of 2001, Jackie and I planned a special trip. We had received a bonus trip when we signed on to a Marriott Time Share in 1999. This was in addition to our regular week and allowed us to make arrangements to stay for one week at any Marriott in the world, free air transportation and a free rental car. Since Jackie had never been to Europe we decided to select one of the cities in Western Europe. Our trip was planned for September and while she wanted to go to Vienna, Austria, we could not get reservations since everything was full for the Oktoberfest and for weeks, preceding it. We then settled on Amsterdam in the Netherlands.

When our daughter learned of our plans, she convinced us that we should not go for just one week, but take advantage of being in Europe to see as much as we could. So we made arrangements to join with a group bus tour out of London. In early September we flew out of Logan Airport in Boston to Ireland. We stayed for 3 days in

Limerick and made day trips, including a trip to Galway Bay. It was while there that we saw our first game of "Hurling" on TV in a small pub. We now understood how people traveling from Europe feel when they encounter the "Super Bowl" in the U.S.

Our stay in Ireland was entirely too short and we promised ourselves that one day we would return to that beautiful isle. Our plane arrived in London where we were to spend the night before embarking on our European bus trip. The following day we met the other passengers (approximately 45) who would be our companions for the next two weeks.

Downtown" Capri

Our 30th anniversary trip to Europe, 2001

There were three nationalities on board: Americans, Canadians and Australians. This was an "over 50" group so we all kept pace with each other. On the first day we traveled to Belgium and as we were disembarking at the hotel and making our way to our rooms Jackie overheard announcements on the TV in the lobby stating that the Pentagon and many other government buildings were being closed to the public

On arriving at our room we quickly turned on the TV just in time to see the second plane strike the Twin Towers in lower Manhattan, N.Y. We were understandably stunned when we realized that this was no movie, it was the real thing! The day was Sept. 11, 2001 and the time was 4:00 p.m. in Brussels… and 9:00 A.M. in New York.

The hours and days that followed were somewhat hectic as we tried to obtain English newspapers to learn more about the tragedy. We called our daughter and she filled us in on some of what happened, also telling us that my nephew, a Lt. Commander in the Navy, had been at the Pentagon that morning earlier but had left just before the explosion there.

As we traveled through Switzerland the next day, we saw buildings draped in black and military personnel with Uzi automatic rifles on every corner. No one really knew if further disasters might occur in other allied countries. We later learned from our tour guide that our itinerary had been somewhat altered to move us from hotels with the word American in their titles. The people everywhere were very kind to us when they learned that we were Americans. Only days later did they realize that many victims of the horror were also from European countries and that this attack was really against the Western Financial powers.

On the Friday after Sept. 11th we were in St. Mark's Square in Venice, Italy. We attended Mass and then seated ourselves in the square to watch the crowds mingle. Shortly, before noon, there was a public address announcement that all over the world there would be a moment of silence for the victims and their families. Along with several thousand other visitors we observed the moment and then a strange thing happened. Jackie was standing next to me and said, "We're Americans! We should have a flag or something to wave." And then, before I knew it, she was singing our National Anthem. I guess she thought others would join her but the crowd just seemed mesmerized listening to her beautiful voice as it grew louder and louder.

When she reached the final stanza, her eyes were closed and tears streamed down her face. Then she opened her eyes and she was surprised to see a huge TV camera focused on her. It was Italian National Broadcast filming her unusual expression of patriotism. (Months later we were meeting with a group of friends at our home and in the course of the conversation, I mentioned this event that took place in St. Mark's Square. One of the women at our meeting let out a squeal and said "then that was you on CNN when they reported what took place around the world after the moment of silence.") So, you never know when you may be singled out for notoriety!!!

The trip was wonderful, for me to see places I had visited on previous trips over a quarter of a century before, and for Jackie to see for the first time. We enjoyed the comfortable friendship of those taking the tour with us and all the interesting sights from the Alps to the Eiffel Tower in Paris.

And then there were the experiences like our evening of opera and dinner in Rome where, once again, Jackie stole the limelight by good-naturedly singing a duet with one of the marvelous male singers. She always seems to be in the right place at the right time.

However our real treat was yet to come. We left the tour group in Calais, France just as they were to board the ship that would take them back to London and then home to the U.S.A. and to their respective countries. We stayed overnight in that quaint city and then boarded a train to take us to Amsterdam the next morning. As we arrived in that city, we looked around for transportation to take us to the Marriott Hotel where we were to spend our free week in the Netherlands. We had loads of luggage which we struggled with boarding the bus that we were told would take us to the plaza in front of the hotel, The bus was crowded and we wondered how we would ever manage to get off at our stop. Everyone spoke English so we told them of our plight. They just smiled and said, "Not to worry!"

When we arrived at our destination, several people left the bus momentarily to help us, and then bid us farewell and good luck. A young girl seeing our confusion stopped by and offered to help us when she heard that we were on our way to the Amsterdam Marriott. She carried our heaviest bags and we followed her doing our best to keep up with her. When we reached the hotel, we tried to offer her something, but she waved us off and smiled as she hurried away.

Almost immediately, there was the doorman and several hotel employees, to take our luggage from us, and usher us into the magnificent hotel lobby. Everyone was smiling and welcoming us at once. We could not have felt more at ease if we had tried. We were about to have the week of our dreams.

We had dinner most nights at the Marriott. The food was superb. Each day, we ventured out to see as much of the country as possible. We would find a place where we could have a light breakfast and then walk or take the trolley, bus or train to our destination. Of course we rode the tour boats on the canals both during the day and again at night.

We also made sure that we got out to Ziendyk to see the famous Dutch windmills that have been preserved for tourists like us to marvel at.

I believe that our most memorable experience (besides dodging thousands of bicyclists, who most assuredly have "the right of way" in Amsterdam.) was our trip out to the city of Arnhem where the World War II academy award winning movie, *A Bridge Too Far*, depicted the valiant yet disastrous effort of British Army forces and a Polish brigade of parachutists to hold one of the many bridges over the Rhine for several days, outnumbered by German troops and panzer divisions attempting to move their army across the Rhine. We walked the restored bridge and read the inscriptions detailing that heroic effort. We then visited the nearby gothic church which was turned into an emergency hospital where the wounded and dying were taken for treatment. A huge glass window depicts what we first thought were hundreds of birds, but on closer inspection we realized that the objects descending were the Polish parachutists.

Of course, we visited the art museums and no trip to Amsterdam would have been complete without a tour of The Heineken Brewery where we sampled ice cold drafts of that delectable beverage. As we left we were presented with an inscribed beer glass as a souvenir.

As we returned to Boston on our transatlantic trip and made our way through the U.S. customs, we were moved to tears by the inspector who asked us how long we had been in Europe. When we told him we were there during "9-11." He said very sadly and simply: "On your return home, you will find a very changed America."

This trip gave me a great opportunity and adequate time to think and reflect on what our next step would be. We had no idea that the trip would leave us more than just fond memories but more importantly a determination to use our callings to serve others while being a part of a larger community. CITI seemed to be the answer to our quest. Here was a group of people who wanted much of what we missed and were also looking for.

Each member of the group pays an annual membership to CITI and receives a card endorsing our membership and stating our current status. Mine reads as follows:

CITI Ministries, Inc. certifies that Reverend James E. Lovejoy is an ordained Catholic priest and member in good standing in the Society of Christ's priesthood, a religious society. He has the authority to perform national and international religious ministries, including marriage ministry, during the year 2006, in accordance with the purpose of CITI Ministries, Inc., a 501c3 nonprofit religious organization chartered in the Commonwealth of Massachusetts, U.S.A.

CITI also has the authorization for ministry from the International Council of Community Churches, which provides authorization for ministry for chaplains requiring such in the armed forces.

There are more than 200 resigned priests working under the auspices of CITI throughout the United States and Canada. Married and other resigned priests provide many different services for a vast number of Catholics who are no longer affiliated with the institutional church, including marriages, baptisms, anointing of the sick and elderly, offering Mass for small assemblies in the spirit of the early Christian communities, and conducting funerals. All of that is done by request from Catholics who either can't or choose not to participate in the institutional church, for whatever reason.

There was great need for that service long before January 2002, but when the truth about pedophile priests and the years of cover-up by many bishops in the United States was first published in the *Boston Globe*, the need became much more evident. Most Catholics, including many priests, had no idea of the epidemic of deviant behavior by Catholic priests entrusted with the care of children. That betrayal of trust was first thought to be an anomaly until word began to spread like wildfire across the nation, implicating one diocese after another.

What angered even the most devout Catholics was the realization that not only had so many priests been guilty of the unthinkable, but their bishops were implicated in encouraging their criminal behavior by failing to report it to the proper authorities and moving the offending priests from parish to parish without warning the faithful that they had probable pedophiles in their midst and that their children were likely to become victims. They even were shown to have ignored or called into question parents or others who demanded the ouster of the predators. Now we know that the first revelations in Boston were just the tip of the iceberg.

One noted psychologist who had worked with those sick men for years was quoted as saying, "If you think that Boston's dilemma was awful, just wait until the truth be known in Los Angeles."

I don't want to paint a picture of a failed celibate priesthood, but in many ways, it's been celibacy that set the stage for the triumphalism that allowed the hierarchy to be so protective of "the good of the Church" that they'd sacrifice even one child to unimaginable abuse at the hands of men using the guise of priesthood to carry out their warped instincts.

Cardinal Law may have escaped prosecution for his behavior and may have been rewarded by the Vatican for his careful protection of his superiors, allowing the institution to appear innocent and free from blame, but one thing must be said in his defense. At least he had the decency, albeit encouraged by some of his own priests, to resign his position as Archbishop of Boston. It's sad to say that no other bishop of the United States has seen fit to follow his lead. Rather, they've entrenched themselves and fought with legal authorities to retain their dubious role as spiritual leaders.

If our actions, as resigned priests, to offer our services to those in need of spiritual help had been suspect prior to those revelations, the church's behavior following exposure by the media more than justified our intervention.

The majority of the Catholic laity has testified, through individual testimony and multiple polls, that a married priesthood is long overdue. I've said on a number of occasions that the laity is far ahead of the hierarchy in grasping the true significance of what has happened and will no longer be the pawns of the clergy—nor will they ever again be satisfied with the admonition that it's the laity's role to pray, pay, and obey.

Shortly after my involvement with CITI, we were fortunate to be given an opportunity to serve as Catholic chaplains on cruise ships over the Christmas and Easter holidays. Our first chaplaincy came during Holy Week of 2002.

We left from Baltimore on Celebrity Cruise Line's *Galaxy*, carrying approximately 2,000 passengers, headed for the Caribbean. Jackie was able to accompany me for a very nominal fee, and it turned out to be a wonderful apostolate.

The crew and the passengers couldn't have been more helpful and appreciative. They knew I was a married priest, but that didn't seem to bother anyone. They were grateful to have a priest on board over Easter.

We went through the long lines like everyone else and were shown to our cabin, which was more than adequate. After the ship got underway, those of us who had special duties on board were asked to meet with the Activities Director. At that time, our duties were spelled out and we had a chance to ask questions. One of the crew members was assigned to work with us to provide religious services during the eleven-day voyage.

We had a great deal of time to ourselves, and the trip was a wonderful vacation. It was late March, so the weather at home was still wintry, but we were headed into Caribbean waters, where it was like midsummer. The decks and pool area were filled with tourists. It was like a little city. I offered Mass each day in a small room set aside for this purpose, explaining beforehand my role as a married priest, but no one seemed to mind. In fact, some people told me they thought it was about time that married priests were recognized by the church.

One couple told us that it was their thirtieth anniversary of marriage, so I asked everyone to pray for them and said I'd be offering that Mass for their special intention. We got to know Lawrence and Olga quite well during the trip, and each year since that cruise, they've asked me to offer Mass for them. They still live in New York, but they recently purchased a second home in South Carolina, and with our move to North Carolina in the fall of 2006, we may get to see them more often.

Anyone who has taken a cruise knows how fabulous the food is on board ship, and it always seems to be available, day and night. Early in Holy Week, we had the occasion to meet a rabbi and his wife. They were on board for the same reason we were, to serve passengers of their faith. They invited us to the Seder meal on Holy Thursday, and we were happy to oblige.

Later in the evening, we had a Holy Thursday liturgy for the Catholics on board and Good Friday services the next day. On Easter

Sunday, we held two Masses and another service for the Protestants. At our Easter morning Mass, approximately 400 attended in the main lounge. Jackie rounded up readers and Eucharistic ministers.

I was apprehensive when I told the people before Mass that I was a married priest and then introduced my wife. I told them that the Mass was valid, but that the church institution didn't recognize us and therefore wouldn't recognize the Mass. I was astounded when the group broke into applause and many stood to show their acceptance. It was the first public Mass I'd offered since I'd left the active ministry in 1971.

I had nearly resigned myself to the realization that I'd never again be able to publicly offer Mass—until I learned of CITI, its endorsement of our priesthood, and its citing of canon law to defend our right (and even obligation) to provide the Eucharist for those who requested it. That Easter 2002 aboard the *Galaxy*, I knew that I hadn't been abandoned by the church as People of God, even if the institution had erased my name and memory from the priestly roster.

The cruise director arranged for us to have a room one afternoon and for us to announce in the daily bulletin that I'd be available to answer questions and explain the reasons for my officiating as a married priest. We thought perhaps we'd have a handful of people show up and that we'd only need the room for about a half hour—but we actually had a room full and had to extend the time to an hour and a half! It was a lively session, and it gave many people an opportunity to ask frank questions, not only about us, but serious questions about the church, as well. (The pedophile abuse scandal had just been uncovered by the *Boston Globe* two months earlier.)

One woman said that she wanted to direct her question to Jackie, and asked about her role as the wife of a married priest. Jackie was forthright, and I believe she cleared up a lot of misconceptions for that woman, and for others in attendance, as well.

Midnight Mass celebrated for our devoted crew in their quarters

The highlight of that cruise (and for that of others to follow) was our opportunity to offer Mass for the crew in the bowels of the ship. Because of their long hours of work, the only free time they had was late at night, so that's when we came to them—and it was a privilege.

Many of the crew members were Catholics from India and South America. They were extremely devout and very grateful that we'd come to them. Some told us that they hadn't had Mass on the ship in more than a year, which made me wonder when the last priest had been aboard and had offered to say Mass for them. They really participated in the Liturgy and Jackie led them in singing. Afterward, almost every crew member came up to us and thanked us for the opportunity to receive God.

One day, a senior officer of the cruise ship called us in our cabin and asked if we'd come to his quarters, where he had gathered some of the other Greek officers. It seemed that a relative had been murdered in Greece, and since they couldn't go to the funeral, they asked if I would hold a small service for them there. Of course, I did and was happy to be of service. It was humbling to see the gratitude on their faces.

Chaplaincy cruise to Alaska, our fantastic waiters on board ship

We had the privilege of serving on two additional cruises—one for Celebrity, and the other on the Norwegian Cruise Line. The second cruise was a double trip to Alaska, and the last cruise was through the Panama Canal. Like the first one, the crews were both very good to us and the people responded warmly, but something had happened at higher levels to cool the enthusiasm of the people in charge.

We were told by CITI that on one cruise (not one on which I had been chaplain) a handful of passengers complained that the priest was married and not truly a priest in their eyes. They had no effect on the other passengers, but when the trip ended, they went to their bishop, who was also a Cardinal in a very influential diocese. Shortly after that, the National Bishops Conference issued a warning to various cruise lines that they should no longer use the services of married priests, telling them that they had some 650 loyal priests who were available to serve as chaplains with institutional endorsement.

That ended our short apostolate to the cruise lines, but we wonder how many Catholics have been deprived of the services of a priest. It seems highly unlikely that the bishops could provide an adequate number of chaplains during two critical periods in the church year, Christmas and Easter, since there's already a dire shortage of priests to serve American parishes. If they're relying on sick, disabled, or retired priests to serve as chaplains, I believe they're doing a disservice to the cruise lines, and it will come back to haunt the hierarchy as the shortage of priests grows over the coming years.

During my married years, my original hope that married priests might one day be invited back to service by a new pope became less and less positive. John Paul II gave no indication during his twenty-five-year pontificate that celibacy would again be optional for Roman Catholic priests. In fact, he made it clear that no bishop worldwide could even discuss such a possibility. I often wonder what St. Peter (who was married) would have to say about that if he were alive today—as well as the priests, bishops, and even popes (two of whom are canonized saints) who were married during the first 1,100 years of the church's existence.

My primary service I've provided during the past four years is to officiate at the marriages of couples who either can't or don't wish to be married in the institutional church. For some, it's simply because they want to be married somewhere other than in a parish church. They may want to be married in a neutral place or outside at their home on a lake. It may be because one of them wished to enter into a second marriage after their first one had deteriorated to the point that there was no longer any semblance of a marriage, despite their good efforts. It may be because they no longer have any faith in the institution or the hierarchy because of the church's behavior. Regardless of the reason, they call upon me because they still believe that they're Catholics and they want some spirituality in their second marriage.

From 2002–06, I've officiated at more than thirty marriages and have fifteen more to officiate this summer. Most of the young couples are in their late 20s or early 30s. They've been dating for an average of four years, have completed college, and have good jobs. They're among the more educated Catholics, and no longer feel that they must follow the strict regulations of the church.

**Fr. Jim solemnizes a wedding with Lake
Winnepausaukee in the background**

All of the marriages I've been privileged to officiate have been special to me and to my wife… and each one has its own special memories. I recall the wedding of one couple a year and a half ago. It took place at the bride's home on a lake in New Hampshire. The beautiful home had belonged to her grandparents and had in recent years been passed down to a second generation. It was special to the bride and groom because they'd spent many wonderful times at that lakeside cottage.

The bride was adamant that she be married there and nowhere else. Her mother told me how happy she and other family members were that they had found me through Rent-a-Priest website.

We held the ceremony at the edge of the lake, while family members and friends spread out on the lawn that rose in tiers to the house. To the surprise and delight of the guests, the father of the bride brought her in on their motor launch and then they walked from the dock to the place where I heard the couple's vows. Many people surrounding the lake knew the family well and brought their boats in close to shore so that they could see and hear the ceremony. When the words pronouncing them husband and wife were uttered, everyone cheered and many sounded their boat whistles and horns. What a dramatic show of support for this couple's future happiness....

Another memory is of a couple whose marriage I officiated in 2004 at the beautiful Nonnatum resort in Kennebunkport, Maine. One of our memories was of their decision to make a donation (instead of providing table favors) to the Children's Cancer unit at the hospital where the bride worked. Another memory was of the groom's elderly but very spry grandmother's acceptance of a married priest at the wedding, despite her Irish Catholic upbringing in Boston.

Baptism of Ella Grace, the child of a couple Jim celebrated 2 years earlier

This Spring I was asked by the same couple to baptize their first child. Of course I told them that it would be a great privilege for me to do so. We had the baptism at their new home in New Hampshire, and once again met many of those who had attended their wedding, in particular the groom's grandmother, who will soon celebrate her

90th birthday. Jackie and I were welcomed by everyone and treated like family by "Grandma."

Jon and Meg's marriage. Father Jim assisted with the mass at Meg's church and delivered the homily

Jeff and Johanna's marriage in the backyard at Sebago, Maine

Extended family, wedding portrait

I was privileged to be involved in both of our son's weddings. I assisted the Episcopal priest when Jon and Meg were married in a solemn Episcopal church wedding in Atlanta, Georgia, blessing the rings and giving a special homily for the occasion. I also officiated at their vows when Jeff and Johanna were married in the beautiful backyard of their home near Sebago Lake, Maine. These were both delightful experiences and ones I'll treasure always. Perhaps that's why my daughter, Jennifer, wanted me to call this book of memories *Many Call Me Father, But My Kids Call Me Dad*.

My children have witnessed the church's hypocrisy in recent years and, like their parents, have been appalled by the revelations of sexual misbehavior of some priests and the inexcusable cover-up by many bishops. They don't hate the church, nor do they blame all priests or bishops for the terrible actions of a few. However, they've lost confidence in the church's authority and intend to follow their own consciences in their marriages and in the education of their own children. (In fact, studies have demonstrated that between sixty and seventy percent of baptized Catholics in the United States no longer practice their Catholic faith on a regular basis.)

The church must accept a giant share of the blame for this condition. Our mission as married priests and members of CITI is simply to respond to estranged Catholics and to insure that they receive the Sacraments they want but have been deprived of by the official church. The institution would like to paint all of us as bad priests who have betrayed our vows and left the priesthood, but nothing could be further from the truth.

We're men who wanted very much to be priests and to provide service. Very few of us ever wanted to promise to be celibate for the rest of our lives. However, in our enthusiasm, we agreed to make such a promise (and for those of us who are diocesan priests, it was a promise and *not* a vow). Then, once we realized that we didn't have the gift of celibacy and wanted to have the love of a woman and to have children of our own, we left the clerical state and married.

Most of us never intended to leave the priesthood. We were validly ordained and once ordained, we could never lose the character of priesthood. Most Catholics applaud our decision and want the church to lift the requirement of celibacy so priests who wish to may marry like any other human being. They believe that the church's ruling, which has stood since the year 1139, should be done away with, and that the church should allow priests to choose to marry—just as it did for more than a thousand years following the death and resurrection of Christ.

They're also aware that at least one of the apostles, and probably more, were married men. They know that not only priests, but many bishops, and even popes, were married during the first millennium of Christianity. They also know something that the church tried to keep secret for years—and that is the fact that more than 100 Protestant ministers who had converted from their former faith indicated a desire to be Catholic priests. Then, by a "Pastoral Provision" granted by the pope, those men were allowed to study for the priesthood—and were ordained. Today, those men serve in various parishes around the country—together with their wives and families!

CHAPTER THIRTEEN
"I AM SO BLESSED"

My intention in writing this short treatise on my life up to this point wasn't to provide a scholarly account, but only to tell in simple, sometimes disjointed, terms what I recall most about my early years growing up, my decision at seventeen to study for the priesthood, my eventual ordination and service as a member of the Roman Catholic clergy for fifteen years, my difficult choice to leave the active ministry and marry without the church hierarchy's permission or blessing, our struggle to find suitable employment and raise three wonderful children, our move from federal employment in Florida and Virginia to become bed-and-breakfast owners in Maine, and finally our decision to reclaim the ministry and under the auspices of the Society of Christ's Priesthood (CITI), to offer spiritual care to those many Catholics and others who have been separated for one reason or another from the institutional church. The most important thing is that my service isn't being thrust upon those people—it's requested by them.

Like most married couples, we've had our ups and downs, joys and disappointments, but we've learned during thirty-five years of married life that it's a special calling, and one that demands far more love, patience, and dedication than any other vocation—including that of the priesthood, and I can say that with some authority, having lived both lives. I know what it is to be a dedicated priest, living a celibate life—and what it is to be a husband, father, and grandfather.

I give credit to those priests who truly believe that they've received the gift (charism) of celibacy and have lived it faithfully and freely. On the other hand, I'd like to have the church give some credit to those of us who realized that a lifetime commitment to celibacy was beyond our calling to the priesthood. Celibacy was forced upon us as a condition of becoming a priest, but it hasn't worked for many of us, not because we were incapable of depriving ourselves of human intimate love with a woman, but because we came to understand and believe that we could and *should* embrace two vocations—which were never intended to be at odds with each other. Why can I not love another human being as my wife and still love and serve the church as People of God? Where is the contradiction?

For most well-informed, educated Catholics today, there's no reason, spiritual or otherwise, for priests to live a life of forced celibacy. To them, it makes no sense to deny only priests something that's the right of all other human beings on Earth. The arguments for celibacy are weak at best—and outrageous at worst.

The church has tried to portray priests as quasi-angelic beings without strong physical attractions to marriage and family, but that's simply not true. It wasn't true for the first human leader of the Christian community, Peter, nor was it true for many other holy popes, bishops, and priests for a thousand years after the Resurrection. The argument that priests are better suited to serve others if they're not burdened with a wife and family ignores and insults the devoted ministers and rabbis of other denominations, as well as doctors, military and political leaders, and heads of corporations, who are as busy as—or even more so—than most priests, yet the majority of them are married and have families.

Finally, the argument that Christ was a celibate and that priests are alter (other) Christ's is almost blasphemous. If the church wants to call the pope the vicar of Peter, that's one thing—but he's not the vicar of Christ. Nobody could have that title, unless he was also God. Priests have a special calling, like the apostles, to follow Christ, but they are not alter Christs.

These and other arguments for celibacy are spurious attempts to give the priesthood an exalted position above the laity, but Christ never inferred as much. Rather, he called the apostles servants of the people. To think otherwise is to cloak priesthood and episcopacy in regal terms—and that is an abomination.

Jim and Jennifer on 'San Francisco trolley' circa 1979

I believe that clericalism (an exaggerated notion that priests deserve special status and privilege) is the real curse of the church today—and always has been. It has driven a wedge between priests and people that's unnatural and absurd. The priests and even some bishops who have resisted that monarchical role have either been ignored by Rome or given minimal authority. One can just imagine how vehemently the Curia (the assembly of Cardinals who advise the pope and hold special places of privilege in the church) must have objected when Pope John XXIII announced after his election as pope that he intended to open the windows of the Vatican and let in some much needed air and light, and then went on to call for the convening of the Second Vatican Council.

We're immensely proud of our three children and thank God for their presence in our lives. As I said earlier, I've never regretted my decision to marry. We've been blessed with a daughter, two sons, two daughters-in-law, and four grandchildren—and I'll always be a priest.

Jennifer is our oldest child.

Jackie likes to tell her that she's our favorite daughter and Jennifer responds, "You mean your favorite *child*, right?"

Born while we lived near the beach, Jennifer means 'Crest of the Wave.' For Jenn, the surf is always up.

All three of our children are very different, as I'm sure is the case in most families, yet they have some things in common. They all have a great sense of social justice. I'd like to think that's partly due to my life—and Jackie's—our combined thirty years of service to the People of God, my work with race relations, and Jackie's teaching in Milwaukee's inner city during the 1960s. The kids are keenly intelligent and very independent, which I can't take credit for—in that way, they resemble their mother.

Jennifer is one of the most generous and thoughtful persons I've ever known. She's sometimes a little too generous for her own good, but I love her for that and wouldn't want her to be any different. She's also the "unifier" in our family. On her own, she brought my brother and his family closer to us, even though they lived miles away. That enabled Jackie and me to be very close to my brother and his wife when George died after a long and difficult illness. Jennifer also helped the members of Jackie's family come closer to us by reaching out to them with genuine love and affection.

Jennifer has probably stayed closer to the Catholic faith than any of us. That's not to say that she doesn't have reservations. She's always searching for a parish or a group she can relate to and find meaning in her faith.

Jackie likes to say that Jennifer, who is single and very beautiful, is "Waiting for an Irish, Catholic democrat who loves *The Sound of Music*." (Her favorite movie.)

Jennifer worked in the business world for a few years after college, but then decided to go back to graduate school, earn her masters' degree, and become an elementary teacher in the Atlanta school system. It's not just a job—it's a true vocation for her, and she's touched many lives during the past ten years, even taking groups of young adults to Europe and Australia during her summer vacations.

Jon is our favorite oldest son.

He's the perfectionist, whether it be in his studies, work, or in sports.

One of his teachers once told Jackie, "Jon will always turn in a perfect assignment, if you wait long enough!"

While given to anger at times, Jon never holds a grudge and is the first to smooth things over. He was always an overachiever, due in part, we believe, to the fact that he skipped a grade early on. He always seemed to be trying to catch up to his class. As an eighth grader, Jon was quarterback for his football team and did well, though he had a hard time seeing over the linemen.

Jim and Jon at Acadia National Park

Although a good student, he became interested in carpentry early on and worked part-time for a local tradesman who taught him the fundamentals of homebuilding. He went on to work with a building crew and worked with other tradesmen, even while he was going to college. He took two years of architecture in college, and while looking for work in Atlanta, Georgia, after graduation, he answered an advertisement and was hired by one of the city's leading homebuilders and renovators.

Jon married an Atlanta girl, Meg Hundley, who also works in the Atlanta school system. They now have a two-and-a-half-year-old son, Jack, who is the apple of their eye. Though they're quite a distance away, we've watched Jack grow, since they send us periodic Internet pictures of his progress.

Family photo at Jon and Meg's wedding

Like many of his peers, Jon lost interest in his Catholic faith after high school, and we noted that his periodic attendance at Mass was usually while he was home on vacation or when we visited him on Parents Weekend at college. Jon and Meg were married in an Episcopal church, and I was invited by the pastor to assist in the ceremony. Jon never criticized the Catholic Church to us, but it was obvious that he'd lost interest. Thanks to Meg, he seems to have had his faith rejuvenated and for that, we're grateful.

Jeff is our favorite youngest child.

I always thought Jeff was going to be the shortest of our three children, but he's now the tallest, and even I find myself looking up to him. Jeff had many friends through the years, though he was always the quiet one. When we went on trips, Jenn and Jon were usually quite vocal, especially toward each other, but we hardly heard much from Jeff. We heard from his teachers, and some of his friends, that Jeff was at the center of everything—sports, class participation, *mischief*—you name it. However, at home he was "the quiet one."

When we first moved to Belfast, Jeff was only nine years old. I went through a period of deep depression at that time, and though he probably doesn't remember, Jeff would often walk with me from our bed-and-breakfast down to the harbor, just so I wouldn't be alone.

We'd usually stay for awhile, watching the ships, and then walk back, stopping at the bakery to get a couple cookies before returning home. He helped me through a tough time in my life.

Our 3rd child 'Jeffrey Edward' 1974

Thank God, We saw the last child graduate from college

Jeff has always loved the sea, at least since we moved to Maine in 1984. During his college summer vacations, he worked on schooners that sailed out of Camden. One year, he invited me to come down to

Rockland and join his ship, *The Mercantile*, during an annual regatta of ships. I remember one incident aboard that ship in particular.

One of the deck hands noted a tear in the mainsail and brought it to the attention of the young captain. The captain turned to Jeff, who was first mate, and asked if he thought he could get up there and fix it. The next thing I knew, Jeff was shinnying up the forty-foot mast. Then he managed to sit up there as he began to repair the torn sail. Meanwhile, a young woman from the galley asked if I wanted to have dinner with the other guests. I told her in no uncertain terms that I'd wait until Jeff got back down to the main deck!

Later, I was introduced to her. Her name was Johanna Peterson, and some years later, she would become Jeff's wife. Jeff and Johanna now have three children: Olivia, almost six, Jonah, almost three, and Pete, our newest addition who is only five months old. We've had the joy of being close enough that they know their Nana and Papa well. They live on Peaks Island, off the coast of Portland, Maine. They all love the island and its simple way of life. They've met many other young couples on the island and enjoy the camaraderie among the residents of that unique community. My wife and I often think that Jeff and Johanna would have loved living in the 1960s, when many young people felt close to the land and sought a less complicated way of life.

They both graduated from Villanova, a Catholic college in Pennsylvania. Jeff now teaches sixth grade Science and Johanna is a nurse. It was at Villanova that Jeff began to question his faith, but he did find relevance in the teachings of philosopher/theologian Chardin and was moved when he heard the social activist Fr. Dan Berrigan speak on campus.

Jeff and Johanna are now searching for a faith that will help them find their place in the universe. Even their marriage, which I officiated, was sublimely simple, taking place in their backyard in Sebago, amid the wonders of nature. I believe that they want God in their lives and in the lives of their children, but not a God that projects fear and retribution. Rather, they're seeking a God that will fill their lives with love—for each other and for all humanity.

Jeff and Johanna's wedding with the extended family

What can we say about our four grandchildren?

First and foremost, I am amazed that I have lived long enough to see and enjoy grandchildren, since I was 43 years old when Jackie and I were married. I once told her that I would be happy if I could see our three children finish high school. But God has seen fit to give me these added years so that I can love and appreciate my children's children.

Olivia is the only girl and she is now 6 years old and has started in the first grade on Peaks Island, Maine, where she lives with her mother, dad and two younger brothers. I doubt that they will ever leave Maine unless Jeff's or Johanna's work requires it.

Their close-to-the-earth life style is shared by most of their neighbors who have an independent spirit that thrives on the island and is unlike many mainlanders.

Olivia, our favorite "first" granddaughter has inherited much of her father's mischievous personality, which goes hand in hand with a deep appreciation of the wonders of nature around her and like him, she is daring in all that she does and yet cares greatly for the people whose lives she touches and who cannot help but be attracted to her.

She also reflects her mother's disposition which is demonstrated by her love of family and her quiet strength in moments of decision-making.

Olivia and her youngest brother, Pete

Olivia is a very intelligent and perceptive child. Jackie is fond of repeating Olivia's description of the occupations of those in our family. She says "my father is a teacher, my mother is a nurse, my Uncle Jon is a builder and my Aunt Jenn and Aunt Meg are also teachers. My grandmother "Mimi" (Johanna's mother) is also a nurse and my Grandpa "Grumpy" (Johanna's father) is a doctor. My Nana (Jackie) is a teacher and (our favorite) **my papa (that's me) helps people get married!"**

Then there is Jonah, Olivia's almost 3 year old brother. Jonah is "perpetual motion." Ever since he could walk Jonah has been on the go just about every waking moment of the day. Everything Olivia does, Jonah wants to do the same thing… only better!! He is impish at times but the next moment very loving. He is really into rockets and space men.

And if you give him something new he hugs it for dear life and carries it around for hours. His parents say that he is a real home body and by that they mean he is not too interested as yet in things outside the home. He is content to just be with his family and the family dog, Daisy.

Olivia, Jonah, and baby Pete

Jeff and Johanna's youngest child, "Pete," is still a baby but he is growing fast and at a little over 4 months he is able to turn himself over completely. Pete is one of the most contented babies I have ever seen. He sleeps and eats and when he is awake and the center of attention he just smiles and smiles and smiles! Olivia and Jonah love their baby brother very much and are the happiest when mother allows them to sit up in a big chair or couch and hold him on their laps.

The Lovejoy Boys, fourth generation, Pete, Jack, and Jonah, July 1, 2006

Our fourth grandchild is "Jack." He is the 2 and a half year old son of Jon and Meg and they live in Atlanta, GA. Jack has always been a lovable child, somewhat on the quiet and serious side, but lots of fun once he gets used to you. Many think Jack looks a great deal like his Dad when Jon was his age, and they believe that Jon and I look alike at the same age and also as young adults, so I guess that says something for heredity.

Nana, Papa, and Jack

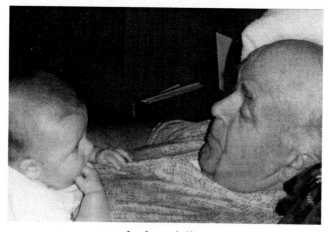

Jack and Jim

Like his father, Jack favors "Yankee" baseball, yet despite that minor fault, we love them both just the same! While Jack is a quiet child, he still has a mind of his own and let's you know it. That is a trait of his father. I think that his warmth and lovable disposition come from both parents but mostly from his mother, Meg, who virtually lights up a room when she enters. Jack's earliest greeting to us on the phone is his one and only, "I wuv vu!!"

Jackie and I love our grandchildren dearly and thank God that He has seen fit to let us live to see each one's uniqueness. He has given us three children who are so different in many ways, yet each one makes us proud to be their parents and our relationship can be summed up in the closing verse of a poem Jennifer gave us years ago, "they know for sure their parents are their dearest friends on earth!!" Amen!!

Thankfully, more good times than bad

EPILOGUE

I asked Jackie to write a few words concerning her feelings about all of this and to share a little of her perspective on our life together. These next few paragraphs will hopefully help to explain how right, even though scary and risky, the choices I made have been for my life and more importantly, the lives of my family.

"My husband is a Catholic priest. To some this may seem very strange and I am asked to explain how this can be. Very simple! Jim left active ministry to marry. He did not leave the priesthood. That is why every year for the last 35 years I have always tried to do something for Jim on Holy Thursday – traditionally the day Christ gave us Holy Orders. Sometimes it may be a card, a special dessert, or a "let's take a ride" after dinner.

My mother and dad never really questioned my marriage after I had left the convent. In fact, my mother asked what she could do to make the day a festive occasion; even going to two florists to satisfy my request for yellow roses and daisies, in cold mid January.

Some of my school friends were surprised at the idea of our marriage. They were pre-Vatican II Catholics. When I went to Wisconsin last summer to visit my mother and sister (who has advanced cancer), some of my school friends had a get-together. My surrogate brother growing up (we met the first day of kindergarten and I had my last date with Bob at a high school dance) asked me at the party, "When, after all these years do I get to meet your Jim?"

Jim and Jackie cutting their wedding cake, 1971

So, my Jim_____ . What does my life with him give me? Jim was and still is a gentleman, opening doors, getting me coffee in the morning, remembering little things I like… occasional flowers, not just on my birthday or our anniversary. Back when we lived in Virginia, Jim would bring me 3 or 4 roses on a Friday after work. He said, "Keep count and remember these flowers on Valentine's Day."

Jim is considerate of me and my need to be me! Jim always gave me space and time when the children were young—suggesting that I go to the Mall after supper and when I would come home, dishes were done and the children were all in bed.

I never felt that I had to ask permission for a visit to Wisconsin to see my mother almost every other year. Jim would just sit back and say, "O.K." When I said that one of our kid's teams needed a chaperone, even an overnight trip for a soccer playoff, he never objected.

As with most marriages we have had our ups and downs, but I find the past few years have been special; growing to love each other in different ways and being in love all over again. Jim has helped me become a more caring person, yet always giving me space and freedom to be me.

In recent years I have been honored to work with Jim in his ministry (which has really become our ministry), sharing my perspectives on marriage and because of my years in Religious Education, my views on education and the Sacraments.

Jim and Jackie 'cruise ministry'

Jim usually ends his homily at marriages with these words from the song we sang at our wedding: "Today is the first day of the rest of your lives!!" And, I know that whenever "Lara's Theme" (the theme song from our first movie date, *Dr. Zhivago*) is heard on the radio when we are traveling in the car, he will turn up the volume. After all these years he is still a "romantic!"

I am blessed to be married to a Catholic priest!!!"

Jacquelyn C. Lovejoy

Now I, Reverend James Edward Lovejoy, married to Jacquelyn C Lovejoy (formerly Kresse), father of three children, grandfather of four children, and for the past fifty years a Roman Catholic priest, bring these thoughts to a close. I have no idea where the Lord will lead us during the ensuing years. However, as long as there's breath in me, I'll continue to use my priesthood in the service of those least appreciated by the hierarchy and will leave it to God's judgment and mercy to decide my reward or punishment for the life I've lead.

I pray that my children will remain close to their mother, who has been such a tower of strength to me for so many years and has always been my best friend. I pray that our children will continue to live tireless lives for their families, friends, and the communities where they live and work. Finally, I pray that those over whom I may have had some influence will intercede for me and my family as we continue to serve a world and a church in turmoil and great need.

One last thought, especially for my family, which is so important to the story of my life. This past Christmas (2005), I told Jackie that I wanted only one gift—a good portrait of our family, including our children, their spouses, and their children. They all planned to be home for the holidays, so I thought it would be the perfect time. After all, who knew when we'd have everyone together again? So Jackie started checking and discovered that one of our neighbors used to be a professional photographer. She said that she'd be delighted to take some pictures, right there in our apartment, so we decided to do that on the Monday after Christmas. The photo is something I will always cherish.

We're immensely proud of them all and feel blessed to have been spared to see them become successful in their personal lives and their chosen vocations. As Jackie and I prepare to leave Maine in October for a warmer climate in North Carolina, we know that we'll miss Jeff and his family and my wonderful New England with its change of seasons, but we look forward to new challenges and a continuation of my work and ministry for whatever time the good Lord sees fit to grant us.

On January 23, 2006, Jackie and I celebrated thirty-five years of marriage, and on June 13th, we attended my sixtieth high school reunion in Saugus, Massachusetts. On June 25th (one day before my seventy-eighth birthday), we joined other members of my Maryknoll class (where I spent the first seven years of my preparation for the priesthood) to commemorate our jubilee year of ordination.

Maryknoll, NY. Jim's 50th anniversary of ordination, June 2006

Finally, on Saturday, July 1, 2006, my wife and our three children surprised me with a party to celebrate my fifty years as a priest. They invited a number of family members and friends to a dinner at the Harraseeket Inn in Freeport, Maine. I was under the impression that I was going there with Jackie to officiate at a marriage renewal ceremony for a close friend.

Friends and family, at surprise party on the occasion of my ordination Jubilee, July 2006

I had never been taken by such complete surprise and once I caught my breath began to recognize people, such as my late brother's family from Chicago and Virginia and close friends from Michigan, Lake Winnepausaukee, New Hampshire, and Belfast, Maine. I was overjoyed. It was a wonderful tribute and I'll remember it for the rest of my life.

My wife and daughter said that I should add some of the comments from people who came to that celebration and from others who couldn't come but sent their best wishes. So, here are a few of those sentiments:

"What you're doing is what Jesus would do. You responded first as a young priest and now as a married priest. You have carved out your place next to Jesus."

"Thanks so much for helping us have the kind of wedding we wished for: spiritual, thoughtful, and fun! Your presence and good humor carried the day."

"Some people are committed to the challenge to walk within His will and to do their part. They're sure to make a difference in the world, because there's such a difference in their heart."

"Thank you so much for sharing in our joy on our wedding day. You made the ceremony warm and caring, exactly what we wanted."

"A priest is someone who knows he/she is blessed and blesses in return. Truly you have been blessed and are a blessing to so many. Your last name (Lovejoy) describes you to a T."

"Thank you, Jim, for many years of friendship shared as fellow innkeepers in Belfast and your presence at Linus' memorial Mass."

"We fondly remember meeting you and Jackie on the Celebrity cruise when we celebrated our thirtieth wedding anniversary. You celebrated Mass for us and officiated as we renewed our vows."

"I'm so honored to be with you today as you celebrate your priesthood. I firmly believe the old saying which surely applies to you: 'Once a priest, always a priest.'"

"I'm forever thankful that you were there for me in 1970 when I converted to Catholicism. It was a big decision and you helped me know it was. I only wish that we had you for our priest right now."

"I wonder, Jim, if you realize what a special place you had in our lives when you were at Newman (UWSP). Your presence was instrumental at the outset of our married life and continues to this day. How could we ever forget that? We can't and we won't. We're grateful forevermore."

"You've been a great friend all of my adult life. Thanks and congratulations!"

"We thank God for you and for all you've done for so many people. Your friendship has meant so much to us."

"Thank you for being such a clear reflection of the love of Jesus for all people."

"We couldn't have asked for a better wedding ceremony than you gave us. Your words and wisdom were a remarkable touch to a joyous occasion."

"One of the greatest things about you is that you've touched so many people's lives. You were there not only for us on our special day, but for so many others, as well. I can't imagine how many people you've helped and supported over the years. We look at the card sent in your honor and see that you've been a part of so many lives both in your own family as well as outside of your family."

I'm grateful to God, to my wife, to my family, and to all those who've had such a profound influence on my life.

Let me close with the words that have allowed me to spend my life in so many different circumstances for others:

Tu es sacerdos in aeternum (thou art a priest forever).

CPSIA information can be obtained at www.ICGtesting.com
Printed in the USA
LVOW080114100512

281073LV00002B/194/A